THE SPIRIT OF CHRISTMAS

CREATIVE HOLIDAY IDEAS
BOOK SEVENTEEN

Christmas is in the air! You can hear it in the merry laughter of children, see it in the evergreen and holly, and feel it in your heart. But all the trappings of the season — the tinsel and colored lights, the tangle of ribbons and wrapping paper, and the whirlwind of social events — are merely a backdrop for the true celebration of Jesus' birth. As you choose from our suggestions for home and party décor, handmade gifts, and menus, we hope that you and your family will find joy, peace, and love in this season of sharing.

LEISURE ARTS, INC.
Little Rock, Arkansas

THE SPIRIT OF CHRISTMAS
BOOK SEVENTEEN

EDITORIAL STAFF
Vice President and Editor-in-Chief: Sandra Graham Case
Executive Director of Publications: Cheryl Nodine Gunnells
Senior Director of Publications: Susan White Sullivan
Director of Designer Relations: Debra Nettles
Publications Director: Kristine Anderson Mertes
Design Director: Cyndi Hansen
Editorial Director: Susan Frantz Wiles
Director of Photography, Public Relations, and Retail Marketing: Stephen Wilson
Art Operations Director: Jeff Curtis
Contributing Photography Director: Lori Ringwood Dimond

DESIGN
Design Manager: Diana Sanders Cates
Designers: Cherece Athy, Tonya Bradford Bates,
    Polly Tullis Browning, Peggy Elliott Cunningham,
    Anne Pulliam Stocks, Linda Diehl Tiano, Becky Werle,
    and Claudia Wendt
Craft Assistant: Lucy Combs Beaudry

FOODS
Foods Editor: Celia Fahr Harkey, R.D.
Technical Assistant: Judy Millard

OXMOOR HOUSE
Editor-in-Chief: Nancy Fitzpatrick Wyatt
Executive Editor: Susan Carlisle Payne
Foods Editors: Allison Long Lowery and Kelly Hooper Troiano
Photographer: Brit Huckabay
Photography Stylist: Ashley J. Wyatt
Contributing Photography Stylist: Connie Formby
Test Kitchens Director: Elizabeth Tyler Luckett
Test Kitchens Assistant Director: Julie Christopher
Recipe Editor: Gayle Hays Sadler
Test Kitchens Staff: Kristi Carter, Nicole L. Faber,
    Kathleen Royal Phillips, Jan A. Smith, Elise Weiss,
    and Kelly Self Wilton

TECHNICAL
Managing Editor: Leslie Schick Gorrell
Technical Writers: Christina Price Kirkendoll,
    Shawnna B. Manes, and Theresa Hicks Young
Technical Associates: Andrea Ahlen,
    Stacey Robertson Marshall, and
    Barbara Marguerite McClintock

EDITORIAL
Managing Editor: Alan Caudle
Senior Editor: Linda L. Garner

ART
Art Publications Director: Rhonda Hodge Shelby
Art Imaging Director: Mark Hawkins
Art Category Manager: Lora Puls
Lead Graphic Artist: Dana Vaughn
Graphic Artists: Chad Brown and Elaine Wheat
Imaging Technician: Mark R. Potter
Photographer: Russell Ganser
Photography Stylists: Janna Laughlin and Cassie Newsome
Publishing Systems Administrator: Becky Riddle
Publishing Systems Assistants: Clint Hanson, Myra S. Means,
    and Chris Wertenberger

PROMOTIONS
Associate Editor: Steven M. Cooper
Direct Mail Designer: Dale Rowett
Graphic Artists: Teresa Boyd and Deborah Kelly

BUSINESS STAFF
Publisher: Rick Barton
Vice President, Finance: Tom Siebenmorgen
Director of Corporate Planning and Development:
    Laticia Mull Dittrich
Vice President, Retail Marketing: Bob Humphrey
Vice President, Sales: Ray Shelgosh
Vice President, National Accounts: Pam Stebbins
Director of Sales and Services: Margaret Reinold
Vice President, Operations: Jim Dittrich
Comptroller, Operations: Rob Thieme
Retail Customer Service Managers: Sharon Hall and
    Stan Raynor
Print Production Manager: Fred F. Pruss

*"... and it was always said of him, that he knew how to keep
Christmas well, if any man alive possessed the knowledge. May
that be truly said of us, and all of us!"*

— From *A Christmas Carol* by Charles Dickens

Library of Congress Catalog Card Number 98-65188
Hardcover ISBN 1-57486-272-3
Softcover ISBN 1-57486-295-2

10   9   8   7   6   5   4   3   2   1

CONTENTS
the *Sights* of Christmas

the *Sights* of Christmas continued

the *Sharing* of Christmas

the *Tastes* of Christmas

the Sights

# of CHRISTMAS

Twinkling lights and
sparkling trims, frosty friends
and crimson blossoms, the
faces of friends and loved
ones gathered to celebrate the
season … these are just a
few of the unforgettable
sights of Christmas. Whether
you prefer traditional or
contemporary style, we can
help you set the stage for
memorable holiday
gatherings.

Natural by Design

Updating your home décor from shades of autumn to winter splendor usually means changing all the decorative elements. But for horticultural designer Chris Olsen, it's an exciting opportunity to blend the two seasons, creating a gloriously natural holiday venue. Come along with this talented artist as he shares a few of his innovative ideas.

Chris decided to keep many elements from the home's autumn décor, replacing fall leaves with evergreens and adding crimson accents and tiny white lights. *(Right)* Twin spruce draw attention to the Bountiful Wreath. Some of the naturals dressing the table were found in nearby woods and fields, and the rest came from the nursery. *(Inset)* Select one of the more unusual pumpkin varieties, such as white "ghost" or fanciful Cinderella pumpkins, to crown a decidedly non-traditional Pumpkin Topiary.

Instructions for Natural by Design *begin on page 138.*

If you love to dig in the garden, don't let winter weather slow you down. This tabletop garden lets you bring a bit of nature indoors. You can use similar techniques to dress the mantel, too!

Instructions for Natural by Design *begin on page 138.*

1. First, cover your table with plastic, then carefully take the plants out of their pots (see page 139 for a listing of the plants Chris used).

2. Use the soil around the trees to create natural-looking hills and valleys, then cover the "terrain" with handfuls of Spanish moss.

3. Nestle smaller ferns and flowering plants among the trees, then disguise the remaining surface with lush green moss mingled with Spanish and deer moss.

4. Make sure the protective plastic is completely covered with moss. For a more natural look, place tufts along the edges, allowing tendrils to trail over the edge.

5. Finally, add candles, ornaments, and any other decorative elements you want ... tiny cabins, animal figures, or a rustic Santa.

6. Be sure to place your candles in clear votive holders or hurricane globes, and never leave them burning unattended.

Rather than one large tree, Chris chose a trio of young cedars and placed them in rustic **Aged Containers**, creating the appearance of a forest grove. Since cedar branches aren't well suited for heavy ornaments, he kept the decorations simple and lightweight, with lots of twinkling lights and matte red balls. If you purchase your trees from a nursery, try keeping the roots intact so you can plant them later; this may be more difficult when digging your own. An informal grouping of gourds, pumpkins, beauty berries, gooseberries, and other natural elements, interspersed with shiny red and gold balls, completes the setting.

More evergreens and pumpkins, along with oversize ornaments, line the steps to the front entrance, which is adorned with a freestyle **Door Swag**. A suggestion from Chris: Don't make your décor too formal ... try for a casual, natural look, and have fun!

Instructions for Natural by Design begin on page 138.

About the Designer

Chris Olsen, a professional landscape designer and owner of Horticare Landscape Management Company, Inc., of Little Rock, Arkansas, is the featured gardening and landscaping expert for a local television station. Turn to page 24 to see how he decorated his own home for the holidays.

Snow
BUSINESS

When you're in the mood
for holiday fun, there's no business
like snow business! You'll bring
in rave reviews with a company
of appealing snowfolk and
frosty accessories.

Set the scene with piles of gaily
wrapped packages, cozy pillows, and
other wintry accents. The colorful felt
Snowman Tree Topper is the star of
the show, with a supporting cast of
handmade and store-bought trims.

Instructions for Snow Business *begin on page 142.*

Our friendly **Snowman Tree Topper** makes a guest appearance on this wreath. It's a snap to make the star-studded tree — simply craft assorted sizes of green **Felt Stars** and glue them to a branch. Wire everything to a ready-made wreath and display it above the mantel with a backdrop of batting "snow," miniature trees, and tiny gifts.

A sparkling pathway of ribbon winds around the evergreen, making its way past bright, easy-to-paint Swirl and Snow-Capped Ornaments, a chorus line of happy **Snowman Ornaments**, a galaxy of golden Felt Stars, and a flurry of fluffy "snowballs."

Instructions for Snow Business begin on page 142.

You can make a whole cast and crew of snow characters to create a festive tableau anywhere! Add personality by varying their scarves and hats. Filled with goodies, the Snowman Gift Holders have the most important roles of all on Christmas morning!

Instructions for Snow Business begin on page 142.

Co-starring on the jolly **Snow Scene Pillow** and **Snowy Tree Skirt**, this happy duo is rated "G" for GREAT! Arrange their arms in different positions to add interest to each panel.

Christmas
Provençal

Prized for its practical elegance and rustic appeal, French provincial décor offers a wealth of holiday inspirations. We selected garden florals and muted shades of Paris green to create this refreshing country setting.

Glowing tapers encircle a basket filled with hydrangea, artichokes, and gooseberries to form the **Candle Centerpiece**, and a simple Matelassé Runner is bordered with ribbon and gimp trim.

Instructions for Christmas Provençal begin on page 146.

On the evergreen, Ivory Decal Ornaments and Pretty Plates feature vintage botanical illustrations, while punched-paper shapes and embossed vellum accent the Beaded Paper Trims. Garlands of gooseberries and sheer ribbon, feather birds, preserved hydrangea, and other purchased trims complement the hand-decorated adornments.

Piles of pretty Embellished Pillows and a cozy Embroidered Chenille Throw issue an unspoken invitation to linger.

Line the shelves of an open cupboard with evergreen, gooseberries, and other natural elements; then fill with treasures such as Berried Topiaries and decorative dishes. We laced wire-edge ribbon through the open borders on some of our plates, and decorated others with floral prints using the decal transfer technique from the tree ornaments. Bottles of flavorful French Country Vinegars look especially appealing capped with wax seals and bead dangles.

Instructions for Christmas Provençal begin on page 146.

Contemporary *Classic*

It's easy to add holiday pizzazz to your contemporary décor! These stylish accents take their cue from the bold, splashy blossoms of a lesser-known Christmas flower … the amaryllis. Luxurious evergreens and ivy, vivacious daisies, and unabashedly oversize ornaments complement the collection.

The mantel sets a tone of sophistication with a pair of Amaryllis-Covered Topiaries and a Floral Wreath (*opposite*), along with various sizes of Amaryllis Globes hung from the ceiling and arrayed on the hearth. (*Right*) Incorporate other favorite florals into a Decorated Tabletop Tree crowned with pheasant feathers and orchids.

Instructions for Contemporary Classic *are on page 151.*

Maximize the architectural features of your home with high-impact details: Eye-catching **Column Swags** make the most of high ceilings, and they're surprisingly lightweight and easy to assemble. *(Below)* Instead of hanging the same old wreaths and bows on the exterior of your home, try something unexpected! Fill gigantic plastic ornaments with faux greenery, nandina berries, and amaryllis and use nylon line to suspend them from the eaves. You'll want to treat the faux berries and flowers with waterproof sealer.

The Amaryllis

Native to the Andes Mountains of South America, the amaryllis reaches the height of its beauty during the winter months. Silk amaryllis are available in shades ranging from snowy white to the classic red used for this collection. Purchase the stems in bulk and enjoy their colorful elegance all through the house.

Don't resign yourself to empty planters during the winter! A basket that holds ferns or trailing vines in warmer weather becomes a brilliant focal point when overflowing with shiny ornaments.

Transform a window box into a Christmas garden with young potted evergreens, such as short-needle pines and blue spruce, which can be planted in the yard later. Select trees that are tall enough to be enjoyed from indoors as well as out, then add real or faux plants and berries to fill in.

Instructions for Contemporary Classic *are on page 151.*

Cookies, Cookies, Everywhere!

It's time for a Christmas cookie exchange! Invite your friends for an afternoon of sampling and swapping favorite recipes … each guest bakes one kind of cookie to bring, then goes home with a delicious variety to share with the family. Turn the page to find fun party tips and yummy recipes, plus creative ideas for packaging take-home goodies.

As the host, you'll want to set a festive table — use your merriest cookie jars and serving platters to showcase treats like **Braided Candy Canes** *(from left)*, Spicy Holiday Fruit Bursts, Nutty Chocolate Bites, **Crescent Sugar Cookies**, Chocolate-Tipped Log Cookies, Holiday Garland Cookies, and **Corner Store Orange Slice Cookies** (recipes on the following pages).

Crescent Sugar Cookies

Chocolate-Tipped Log Cookies

Party Tips

1. Limit the number of guests to 8 or less. Remember, everyone's going to have to bring enough cookies to send home with each guest, plus cookies for snacking at the party!

2. Enclose plenty of decorated recipe cards with your invitations so guests can write out their recipes to share.

3. Request RSVP's! Find out what cookies your friends are bringing so you can make "place cards" ahead of time to identify each type of goody on the buffet table.

4. Provide plenty of beverages such as coffee, cider, cocoa, and punch. You'll also want to serve a few salty snacks to balance all the sweets!

CHOCOLATE CAPPUCCINO COOKIES

 2 cups butter or margarine, softened
 4 cups firmly packed light brown sugar
 4 large eggs
5¹/₂ cups all-purpose flour
 1 cup baking cocoa
¹/₄ cup instant coffee granules
 1 teaspoon baking powder
 1 teaspoon baking soda
 1 teaspoon salt
 1 package (10 ounces) cinnamon baking chips

Beat butter at medium speed with an electric mixer until creamy. Gradually add brown sugar, beating well. Add eggs, beating until blended. Combine flour and next 5 ingredients. Gradually add to butter mixture, beating at low speed just until blended. Stir in cinnamon chips. Drop dough by rounded tablespoonfuls, 2 inches apart, onto lightly greased baking sheets. Bake at 350°, in batches, for 8 to 10 minutes. Cool on baking sheets 5 minutes. Remove to wire racks to cool completely.
Yield: about 8 dozen cookies

Instructions for Cookies, Cookies, Everywhere!
begin on page 152.

Who could resist mouth-watering morsels like pretty Holiday Garland Cookies, yummy iced Corner Store Orange Slice Cookies (recipes on page 36), and Chocolate Cappuccino Cookies packed with cinnamon baking chips (recipe opposite)? Decorative papers and scrapbooking stickers make it easy to craft the adorable cookie Place Cards!

Holiday Garland Cookies

Chocolate Cappuccino Cookies

CRANBERRY-ALMOND SUPREMES

These cookies can be baked ahead and frozen up to 6 months.

- 1 cup butter, softened
- 3/4 cup sugar
- 3/4 cup firmly packed light brown sugar
- 1/2 teaspoon almond extract
- 2 large eggs
- 2 1/4 cups all-purpose flour
- 1 teaspoon baking powder
- 1 teaspoon salt
- 2 cups chopped fresh cranberries
- 1 cup slivered almonds, toasted

Beat butter at medium speed with an electric mixer until creamy; gradually add sugars, beating well. Add almond extract and eggs, beating until blended. Combine flour, baking powder, and salt; gradually add to butter mixture, beating at low speed until blended after each addition. Stir in cranberries and almonds. Drop by rounded tablespoonfuls onto ungreased baking sheets. Bake at 375° for 9 to 11 minutes. Remove to wire racks to cool.
Yield: about 3 1/2 dozen cookies

SPICY HOLIDAY FRUIT BURSTS

- 3 1/2 cups all-purpose flour
- 2 teaspoons baking powder
- 1 teaspoon ground cinnamon
- 1/2 teaspoon salt
- 1/2 teaspoon ground nutmeg
- 1 cup shortening
- 2 cups firmly packed brown sugar
- 2 large eggs
- 1/2 cup milk
- 1 cup chopped pecans
- 1 cup chopped dates
- 1 cup chopped candied cherries
- 1/2 cup uncooked old-fashioned oats
  Red or green whole candied cherries, halved (optional)

Combine first 5 ingredients; set aside. Cream shortening; gradually add brown sugar, beating until light and fluffy. Add eggs; beat well. Add dry ingredients alternately with milk, beating well. Stir in next 4 ingredients. Drop dough by level tablespoonfuls onto ungreased baking sheets. Top each cookie with a cherry half. Bake at 375° for 10 to 12 minutes. Cool on wire racks.
Yield: about 6 1/2 dozen cookies

Instructions for Cookies, Cookies, Everywhere! begin on page 152.

COCONUT-MACADAMIA DELIGHTS

- 1/2 cup sugar
- 1/2 cup firmly packed light brown sugar
- 1/2 cup butter or margarine, softened
- 1 large egg
- 1 teaspoon vanilla extract
- 1 1/4 cups all-purpose flour
- 1 cup uncooked quick-cooking oats
- 1/2 cup flaked coconut
- 1/2 teaspoon baking soda
- 1/4 teaspoon salt
- 1 cup coarsely chopped macadamia nuts

Beat first 5 ingredients at medium speed with an electric mixer until fluffy. Combine flour and next 4 ingredients. Add half of mixture at a time to sugar mixture, beating at low speed until blended; stir in nuts. Drop dough by heaping teaspoonfuls, 2 inches apart, onto lightly greased baking sheets. Bake at 350° for 7 to 10 minutes or until edges are golden brown. Cool on baking sheets 1 minute. Remove to wire racks to cool.
Yield: about 3 dozen cookies

OLD-FASHIONED CHRISTMAS SPICE COOKIES

    1   cup butter or margarine, softened
    3/4 cup sugar
    1 1/2 tablespoons dark molasses
    2   teaspoons ground cinnamon
    1/2 teaspoon ground cardamom or ginger
    1   tablespoon water
    1   teaspoon baking powder
    2 1/2 cups all-purpose flour
    1   egg white, lightly beaten
         Sugar

Beat butter at medium speed with an electric mixer until creamy. Add 3/4 cup sugar, beating until smooth. Add molasses, cinnamon, and cardamom, beating until blended. Combine 1 tablespoon water and baking powder, stirring until baking powder is dissolved; add to butter mixture. Gradually add flour to butter mixture, beating until blended. Turn dough out onto a lightly floured surface; roll to 1/4-inch thickness. Cut with a 1 1/2-inch round cookie cutter (or size to fit your tumbler). Place, 2 inches apart, on lightly greased baking sheets. Brush evenly with egg white; sprinkle with sugar. Bake at 375° for 8 minutes or until lightly browned. Cool on baking sheets 5 to 6 minutes. Remove to wire racks to cool completely.

Yield: about 7 dozen cookies

NUTTY CHOCOLATE BITES

    1   cup water
    1/2 cup butter or margarine
    1/2 cup vegetable oil
    2   cups all-purpose flour
    2   cups sugar
    1/4 cup cocoa
    1/2 cup buttermilk
    1   teaspoon baking soda
    2   large eggs, beaten
         Fudge Frosting
    1/2 cup chopped peanuts

Combine water, butter, and oil in a small saucepan; bring to a boil. Combine flour, sugar, and cocoa in a mixing bowl; add hot mixture, stirring well. Combine buttermilk and soda; stir until soda dissolves. Add buttermilk mixture and eggs to batter; mix well. Spoon mixture into a greased 15 x 10-inch jellyroll pan. Bake at 400° for 15 minutes.

Frost brownies with Fudge Frosting while warm; sprinkle with peanuts. Cool; cut into squares.

Yield: about 3 dozen bars

FUDGE FROSTING

    1/2 cup butter or margarine
    1/3 cup buttermilk
    1/4 cup cocoa
    1   package (16 ounces) powdered sugar, sifted
    1/2 teaspoon vanilla extract

Combine butter, buttermilk, and cocoa in a medium saucepan; bring to a boil. Remove from heat. Add powdered sugar and vanilla; blend until smooth.

Don't send those merry masterpieces home in plain old plastic bags! You and your guests will have fun crafting whimsical Santa Pins to fasten ribbon-tied bags of Spicy Holiday Fruit Bursts. And it's super-simple to dress up plain tumblers to hold Old-Fashioned Christmas Spice Cookies — just apply stickers and borders (the ones with a clear background work best).

Party Tip

Don't limit your party to just one room! Set up "conversation nooks" in different areas — the living room, the kitchen, the study, etc. — so your friends can enjoy more of your holiday décor.

To make festive little packages, tie stacks of **White and Dark Chocolate Dreams** with cheery craft ribbon and add a minty treat.

COCONUT LACE COOKIES

    2 tablespoons hot water
1 1/2 teaspoons baking soda
  3/4 cup butter or margarine, melted
    1 tablespoon light corn syrup
1 1/2 cups uncooked old-fashioned oats
1 1/2 cups firmly packed light brown sugar
1 1/2 cups all-purpose flour
1 1/2 cups sweetened flaked coconut

Stir together hot water and soda in a large bowl until soda dissolves. Add butter and corn syrup, stirring until blended. Combine oats and next 3 ingredients; stir into butter mixture, stirring until blended. Shape dough into 3/4-inch balls, and place, 3 inches apart, on lightly greased baking sheets. Slightly flatten dough balls. Bake at 350° for 7 to 8 minutes or until golden brown. Remove to wire racks to cool.

Yield: about 2 dozen cookies

BUTTERSCOTCH-PECAN BROWNIES

  2/3 cup butter or margarine, softened
1 1/2 cups firmly packed brown sugar
    2 large eggs
    2 teaspoons vanilla extract
    2 cups all-purpose flour
    1 teaspoon baking powder
  1/4 teaspoon baking soda
    1 teaspoon salt
    1 cup butterscotch morsels
  1/2 cup chopped pecans

Cream butter; add brown sugar, beating well. Add eggs and vanilla to mixture, beating well. Combine flour, baking powder, soda, and salt; add to creamed mixture, stirring well. Pour batter into a greased 13 x 9-inch baking pan. Sprinkle with butterscotch morsels and pecans. Bake at 350° for 30 minutes. Cool; cut into bars.

Yield: about 2 1/2 dozen bars

CRESCENT SUGAR COOKIES

    1 cup butter or margarine
    2 cups all-purpose flour
  3/4 cup sour cream
    1 egg yolk
  3/4 cup sugar
  3/4 cup chopped pecans
    1 teaspoon ground cinnamon

Cut butter into flour with a pastry blender until mixture resembles coarse meal. Add sour cream and egg yolk, stirring until flour mixture is moistened. Divide dough into 5 equal portions; chill several hours.

Combine sugar, pecans, and cinnamon; set aside. Roll each dough portion into an 8-inch circle on a floured surface; sprinkle with sugar mixture. Cut circle into eighths. Roll up each wedge, starting at wide end; seal points firmly. Place on ungreased baking sheets, point side down. Bake at 350° for 20 minutes or until lightly browned. Remove to wire racks to cool.

Yield: 40 cookies

CHOCOLATE CHIP-PEANUT BUTTER SQUARES

  1/3 cup butter or margarine, melted
  1/2 cup sugar
  1/2 cup firmly packed light brown sugar
  1/2 cup chunky peanut butter
  1/2 teaspoon vanilla extract
    1 large egg, beaten
  1/4 cup milk
1 1/2 cups all-purpose flour
  1/2 teaspoon baking soda
  1/2 teaspoon salt
    1 package (6 ounces) semisweet chocolate morsels

Combine first 7 ingredients, mixing well. Combine flour, soda, and salt; add dry ingredients and chocolate morsels to peanut butter mixture, stirring well. Pour batter into a greased 9-inch square pan. Bake at 375° for 25 minutes. Cool completely; cut into squares.

Yield: about 3 dozen bars

WHITE OR DARK CHOCOLATE DREAMS

- ³/₄ cup shortening
- ³/₄ cup butter, softened
- 2¹/₄ cups sugar
- 3 large eggs
- 1¹/₂ teaspoons vanilla extract
- 6 ounces white or semisweet chocolate, melted and cooled
- 5³/₄ cups all-purpose flour
- 2¹/₄ teaspoons baking powder
- 1¹/₂ teaspoons salt

Beat shortening and butter at medium speed with an electric mixer until creamy; gradually add sugar, beating well. Add eggs and vanilla, beating until blended. Stir in melted chocolate. Combine flour, baking powder, and salt. Add flour mixture to butter mixture, beating at low speed until thoroughly combined. Divide dough into fourths; chill 1 hour.

Turn dough out onto lightly greased aluminum foil; roll to ¹/₄-inch thickness with a lightly floured rolling pin, or cover dough with plastic wrap and roll out. Transfer aluminum foil with dough to a baking sheet. Make horizontal and vertical cuts in dough every 2 inches, using a pizza cutter. Do not remove dough squares; only remove excess dough along edges. Bake at 350° 10 to 12 minutes or until bottom of cookies are golden brown. Cool on baking sheets 2 minutes; recut using pizza cutter. Remove to wire racks to cool.

Yield: about 7 dozen cookies

BRAIDED CANDY CANES

- ³/₄ cup butter or margarine, softened
- 1 cup sugar
- 3 large eggs
- 1 tablespoon vanilla extract
- 4 cups all-purpose flour
- 1 tablespoon baking powder
- ¹/₂ teaspoon baking soda
  Vegetable cooking spray
  Red decorator sugar crystals or sesame seeds

Beat butter at medium speed with an electric mixture until soft and creamy; gradually add sugar, beating well. Add eggs and vanilla, mixing well. Combine flour, baking powder, and soda; gradually add flour mixture to butter mixture, mixing at low speed just until blended. Divide dough into fourths. Divide each fourth of dough into 14 portions. Roll each portion into an 8-inch rope; place two ropes together and twist. Shape twists into candy canes, lightly coat with cooking spray, and sprinkle with sugar crystals or sesame seeds. Place cookies, 2 inches apart, on lightly greased baking sheets; bake at 350° for 10 to 12 minutes or until the edges begin to brown. Remove to wire racks to cool.

Yield: 2¹/₄ dozen cookies

Jolly Painted Mugs are perfect for holding long, narrow cookies like these sugar-sprinkled **Braided Candy Canes.**

Instructions for
Cookies, Cookies, Everywhere!
begin on page 152.

GRANDMA'S CLASSIC SUGAR COOKIES

1 cup butter, softened
1 cup sugar
1 large egg
3 1/2 cups all-purpose flour
1 1/4 teaspoons baking powder
1/8 teaspoon baking soda
1/2 teaspoon ground cinnamon
1/2 teaspoon ground nutmeg
Decorating sugar

Cream butter; gradually add 1 cup sugar, beating until light and fluffy. Add egg; beat well. Combine flour, baking powder, soda, cinnamon, and nutmeg; add to creamed mixture, mixing until blended. Cover and chill dough.

Work with one fourth of dough at a time; store remaining dough in refrigerator. Place dough on a lightly greased baking sheet; roll out to 1/4-inch thickness. Cut dough with floured cookie cutter, leaving 1 to 2 inches between each cookie. Remove excess dough from baking sheet; combine with remaining dough in refrigerator. Repeat procedure with remaining dough. Sprinkle cookies with decorating sugar before baking. Bake at 350° for 10 to 12 minutes or until cookies are lightly browned. Cool on baking sheets 3 to 5 minutes; remove from baking sheets, and cool completely on wire racks. Repeat procedure with remaining dough.
Yield: about 6 1/2 dozen cookies

HOLIDAY GARLAND COOKIES

1 cup butter, softened
1 cup sifted powdered sugar
2 large eggs, separated
1/2 teaspoon vanilla extract
2 1/4 cups all-purpose flour
1/8 teaspoon salt
Red and green candied cherries

Cream butter; gradually add powdered sugar, beating well. Add egg yolks and vanilla; mix well. Stir in flour and salt. Cover and chill at least 1 hour.

Shape 1 tablespoon dough into a 6-inch rope. Place rope on a lightly greased baking sheet, bringing ends of rope together to form a circle; pinch ends together to seal. Repeat with remaining dough. Slightly beat egg whites; carefully brush each cookie with egg whites where cherries will be placed. Decorate with pieces of red and green candied cherries. Bake at 350° for 10 to 12 minutes or until lightly browned. Remove to wire racks to cool.
Yield: about 2 1/2 dozen cookies

CORNER STORE ORANGE SLICE COOKIES

3/4 teaspoon baking soda
1 1/2 tablespoons water
1 cup shortening
1 cup firmly packed light brown sugar
1/2 cup sugar
2 large eggs
10 orange candy slices, chopped
3/4 cup chopped pecans
1/2 cup flaked coconut
2 cups all-purpose flour
1 1/2 cups uncooked quick-cooking oats
3/4 teaspoon baking powder
2 cups powdered sugar
1/4 cup orange juice

Stir together soda and 1 1/2 tablespoons water until dissolved. Beat shortening at medium speed with an electric mixer until creamy. Gradually add sugars, beating until fluffy. Add soda mixture, eggs, and next 3 ingredients; beat until blended. Combine flour, oats, and baking powder. Gradually add to shortening mixture, beating until blended. Drop by rounded tablespoonfuls onto lightly greased baking sheets. Bake cookies at 350° for 10 to 12 minutes. Remove to wire racks to cool.

Stir together powdered sugar and orange juice; drizzle over cookies.
Yield: about 4 dozen cookies

MAKE-AHEAD STRAWBERRY BUTTER COOKIES
Make ahead and freeze.

1 1/2 cups butter, softened
1 1/4 cups sugar
1 large egg
1 teaspoon vanilla extract
2 cups all-purpose flour
3/4 cup strawberry preserves

Beat butter and sugar at medium speed with an electric mixer until fluffy. Add egg and vanilla, beating well. Add flour, beating just until mixture is blended. Divide dough into 3 portions; roll each portion on wax paper into a 12-inch log. Cover and chill 8 hours.

Cut each log into 1/2-inch-thick slices; place on lightly greased baking sheets. Press thumb in center of each slice to make an indentation; fill with 1/2 teaspoon preserves. Bake at 350° for 10 minutes or until edges are lightly browned. Remove to wire racks to cool.
Yield: about 6 dozen cookies

CHOCOLATE-TIPPED LOG COOKIES

1 cup butter or margarine, softened
$^1/_3$ cup sugar
2 teaspoons brandy
2 teaspoons vanilla extract
$^1/_4$ teaspoon salt
2 cups all-purpose flour
2 cups chopped pecans
   Sifted powdered sugar
6 ounces chocolate-flavored candy coating, melted

Cream butter; gradually add sugar, beating until light and fluffy. Add brandy, vanilla, and salt, mixing well. Add flour, stirring until blended; stir in pecans. Shape dough into $1^1/_2$ x $^1/_2$-inch logs. Place, 2 inches apart, on ungreased baking sheet. Bake at 325° for 15 to 20 minutes (cookies should not brown). Remove to wire racks to cool.

Lightly roll cookie logs in powdered sugar while slightly warm. When cookies are completely cool, dip one end in melted candy coating. Let stand on wax paper until set.
Yield: about 6 dozen cookies

Send guests home with lasting memories of your get-together: To help your friends carry their packages of cookies home, paint plain, inexpensive wooden serving trays white, then add checkerboard and polka-dot borders — so simple to do, yet so special!

Woodland Wonder

Let your holiday spirit take flight! With just a few basic elements, you can craft trims to bring natural woodland glory to any room.

Showcasing a colorful cardinal, this **Appliquéd Pillow** is too pretty to pack away after Christmas — and you don't have to! Leave it out for everyone to enjoy all winter long.

Instructions for Woodland Wonder begin on page 154.

It's simple to add gilded highlights to plain grapevine stars or pinecones ... just dry-brush the raised surfaces with metallic paint.

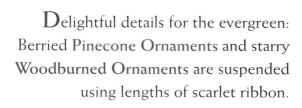

Delightful details for the evergreen: Berried Pinecone Ornaments and starry Woodburned Ornaments are suspended using lengths of scarlet ribbon.

All of our **Woodland Garlands,** including the mini swag over the mantel, can be made following one set of basic instructions using your choice of greenery and other elements. Atop the mantel, candles perch in "nests" made by shaping dried vines into rings and adding bits of berry garland. *(Below)* A **Candle Wreath** adds a festive touch to a side table.

Instructions for Woodland Wonder begin on page 154.

I heard a bird sing
In the night of December
A magical thing
And sweet to remember.

"We are nearer to Spring
Than we were in September,"
I heard a bird sing
In the dark of December.

— Oliver Herford

And it came to pass in those days, that there went out a decree from Caesar Augustus that all the world should be taxed. (And this taxing was first made when Cyrenius was governor of Syria.) And all went to be taxed, every one into his own city. And Joseph also went up from Galilee, out of the city of Nazareth, into Judaea, unto the city of David, which is called Bethlehem; (because he was of the house and lineage of David) to be taxed with Mary, his espoused wife, being great with child. And so it was, that, while they were there, the days were accomplished that she should be delivered. And she brought forth her firstborn son, and wrapped him in swaddling clothes, and laid him in a manger; because there was no room for them in the inn.

— *Luke 2:1-7, King James Version*

A *Night* TO REMEMBER

In the midst of the hectic holiday preparations, it's nice to pause and remember the events of that holy night so long ago. Give the crèche a place of honor in your home.

To add a bronze patina to an inexpensive plaster urn, see our painting technique on page 181. To begin, fill the urn with floral foam and cover it with sheet moss. Arrange greenery over the moss (we used juniper, ivy, and frosted grapes), using hot glue and floral pins to hold it in place. To make a grapevine dome, bend a length of copper tubing to form an arch and place it in the urn. Inserting ends of vines into foam and securing with wire, loosely attach grapevine along the tubing; then add lengths running from the edge of the urn to the center of the arch. Finish with greenery and rustic stars, if you like. Now, place your Nativity figures in their beautiful new setting and enjoy!

Chocolate Fantasies

Indulge chocolate lovers
with a holiday gathering devoted
entirely to the "food of the gods!"
Along with serving traditional chocolaty
desserts and goodies, you can also
make beautiful table decorations
and favors from luscious,
oh-so-wonderful chocolate!

For delectable greetings, place an edible
Chocolate Place Card, with the guest's
name piped in frosting, at each setting.
Gourmet gifts: fill fanciful (but amazingly
easy to make) Chocolate Treat Boxes
with your choice of homemade or
purchased confections — shiny dragées
are elegant decorations.

These chocolate projects can be made with candy coating, baking chocolate, or tempered chocolate (see page 51). The candy coating is more stable than baking chocolate, but has less flavor. The tempered chocolate retains the chocolate flavor and will remain shiny and smooth without chocolate bloom or discoloration.

CHOCOLATE TREAT BOXES
Use candy bars with imprinted sections for easy cutting of the "walls" of the boxes.

Small and Large Square Boxes
2 dark or milk chocolate bars (about 1.5 ounces each)
Chocolate Frosting
Gold dragées (see Note)

Oval Boxes
16 ounces chocolate-flavored candy coating
Chocolate Frosting

For small boxes with a bottom, cut chocolate bars into five 1³/₈-inch squares (or any size that works with your candy). For large boxes, cut candy bars into four pieces measuring 2³/₄ x 2¹/₈ inches (or any size that works with your candy). For oval boxes, melt candy coating according to package directions in a small saucepan. Pour into an ungreased, 4¹/₄ x 3-inch plastic egg-shaped candy mold. Chill 10 to 15 minutes until the outer ¹/₄ inch is solid. Pour coating that has not hardened out of the mold. Return mold to refrigerator; chill 5 minutes to completely harden. Smooth exposed upper edges with a warm metal spatula; chill.

Spoon Chocolate Frosting into a pastry bag fitted with a small round tip. With smooth sides of candy bars facing out, use frosting to "glue" sides of square boxes together, then "glue" onto bottom piece, if using. Allow frosting to harden.

To decorate, pipe frosting onto each box and press dragées into frosting, as desired.
Yield: 1 small or large square box, 1 oval box
Note: Gold dragées are nonedible and recommended for decoration only.

CHOCOLATE PLACE CARD
2 ounces vanilla-flavored candy coating
5 dark or milk chocolate bars (about 1.5 ounces each)
Chocolate Frosting

Melt candy coating according to package directions. Pour into ungreased, plastic holly leaf-shaped candy molds; clean edges of molds. Chill 5 to 10 minutes or until candy hardens. Tap mold onto wax paper to release candies. Spoon Chocolate Frosting into a pastry bag fitted with a small round tip. Pipe name and decorative trim onto flat side of chocolate bars. Use frosting to "glue" candy leaves to place cards.
Yield: 5 place cards

CHOCOLATE FROSTING
Use semisweet or white chocolate chips depending on the decorative look that you want.

1 cup (6 ounces) chocolate chips
2 tablespoons butter
2 cups sifted powdered sugar
3 to 4 tablespoons milk

Combine chocolate and butter in a medium saucepan. Stirring constantly, melt chocolate over low heat. Remove from heat. Add powdered sugar and 3 tablespoons milk; beat at high speed of an electric mixer until smooth. Add additional milk for desired consistency.
Yield: 1¹/₂ cups frosting

TIERED CANDY PLATE
You'll need a ¹/₄-inch wooden dowel and cardboard cutouts to make the candy plate stable.

1 cup butter or margarine, softened
1¹/₂ cups powdered sugar
1 egg
1 teaspoon vanilla extract
2 cups all-purpose flour
¹/₂ cup cocoa
¹/₂ teaspoon salt
1 cup powdered sugar
1 tablespoon meringue powder
2 to 3 tablespoons cocoa
2 tablespoons water
Candies

Beat butter and powdered sugar until fluffy. Add egg and vanilla; beat until smooth. Combine flour, cocoa, and salt; add to creamed mixture. Stir until a soft dough forms. Cover; chill 1 hour.

Turn dough onto a lightly floured surface; roll to ¹/₄-inch thickness with a lightly floured rolling pin. Use 4¹/₈-, 4³/₄-, 5¹/₄-, and 7³/₄-inch star-shaped cookie cutters to cut 1 cookie each for tiers, and a 2-inch round cookie cutter to cut 12 cookies for spacers. Place on lightly greased baking sheets. Bake at 375° for 5 to 10 minutes or until bottoms are lightly browned. Remove to wire racks. While cookies are warm, use a ¹/₄-inch dowel to punch a hole through center of each cookie except the smallest star cookie. Cut 2 pieces of cardboard ¹/₂ inch smaller than the 5¹/₄- and 7³/₄-inch cutters to support cookies. Stack cookies onto dowel before icing, placing the cardboard under the 5¹/₄- and 7³/₄-inch cookies. Mark dowel so that the top is flush with the last stacked round cookie. Unstack cookies and cut dowel at mark. In a small bowl, beat powdered sugar, meringue powder, cocoa, and water with an electric mixer 7 to 10 minutes or until icing is stiff. Restack cookies using dowel and cardboard; apply icing between cookies to hold together. Allow icing to set up before placing candies on tiers.
Yield: 1 tiered plate

CHOCOLATE STAR SUCKERS

6 ounces white chocolate, finely chopped
6 ounces dark chocolate, finely chopped
6 sucker sticks

Temper white and dark chocolates (see Tempering Chocolate, page 51). Cool to proper temperature. Drop spoonfuls of white and dark chocolate into lightly greased 3½-inch star-shaped sucker molds; do not overfill. Lightly swirl chocolates with a knife; clean edges of molds. Insert sucker sticks. Chill for 15 minutes or until hardened. Tap mold on wax paper to release suckers.

Yield: 6 suckers

Partygoers will find this **Tiered Candy Plate** simply irresistible! Be sure to bake plenty of extra cookies for snacking, or else you may catch nibblers munching on the star-shaped "plates!" Wrap marbled **Chocolate Star Suckers** in cellophane for heavenly party favors.

CHOCOLATE-DIPPED WAFFLE CONES

Use short drinking glasses to hold cones upright while the chocolate is hardening.

- 12 waffle cones
- 1 pound semisweet chocolate, finely chopped
- 4 ounces white chocolate, finely chopped,
    OR brown edible glitter
    OR chocolate-flavored sprinkles

Temper semisweet chocolate (see Tempering Chocolate, page 51). Dip open ends of cones into chocolate; lightly shake to remove excess chocolate. Place cones upright in glasses. To decorate with glitter or sprinkles, immediately sprinkle cones before chocolate sets up; allow chocolate to harden. To decorate with white chocolate, allow chocolate-dipped cones to harden. Temper white chocolate; drizzle onto cones. Place cones upright in glasses; allow chocolate to harden.

Yield: 12 cones

CHOCOLATE MOUSSE

Pipe or spoon Chocolate Mousse into Chocolate-Dipped Waffle Cones or Chocolate Treat Boxes (page 46).

- 2¹/₂ cups whipping cream, divided
- ¹/₄ cup sugar
- 4 egg yolks, beaten
- 6 ounces semisweet chocolate, finely chopped

In a medium saucepan, combine 1 cup cream and sugar. Stirring frequently, cook over medium heat until mixture begins to simmer. Reduce heat to low. Slowly whisk some of the hot mixture into eggs. Whisking constantly, add egg mixture back into saucepan; cook until mixture coats the back of a spoon. Remove from heat; strain into a medium bowl. Cool 5 minutes. Add chocolate; stir until melted and mixture is smooth. Beat remaining whipping cream in a chilled bowl until stiff peaks form. Fold into chocolate mixture; chill.

Yield: 4¹/₂ cups mousse

Dusted with sparkling edible glitter, **Cocoa Meringue Snowflakes** are almost (but not quite) too pretty to eat! They're lovely additions to your cookie tray, or you can use ribbon to attach them to garlands or hang them on the tree — or even the chandelier! Serve our grown-up version of a favorite childhood treat: decorate **Chocolate-Dipped Waffle Cones** with candy sprinkles, edible glitter, or drizzles of white chocolate, then fill them with luscious **Chocolate Mousse**.

COCOA MERINGUE SNOWFLAKES

- 1¼ **cups powdered sugar**
- 3 **tablespoons cocoa**
- ½ **teaspoon cream of tartar**
- ½ **teaspoon ground cinnamon**
- 4 **egg whites**
- 1 **teaspoon almond extract**
  Gold dragées (see Note)
  White edible glitter

Trace snowflake pattern (page 177) onto tracing paper. Place on baking sheet. Cover tracing paper with wax paper. Sift powdered sugar, cocoa, cream of tartar, and cinnamon together. In a large bowl, beat egg whites until foamy. Add almond extract and dry ingredients; beat at high speed with an electric mixer until very stiff peaks form. Spoon meringue, about ¼ cup at a time, into a pastry bag fitted with a medium round tip; place remaining meringue in refrigerator until ready to use. Pipe meringue onto wax paper following the snowflake pattern, moving the pattern as necessary. Decorate with gold dragées and edible glitter. Bake at 200° for 2 hours. Leaving meringues on wax paper, remove from baking sheet to wire rack while cookies are still warm; cool completely. Carefully remove wax paper. Store in an airtight container.
Yield: about 2 dozen meringues
Note: Gold dragées are nonedible and recommended for decoration only.

Crowned with a lovely filigree star and trimmed with golden dragée "ornaments," this **Chocolate Cookie Tree** is a stunning centerpiece, whether you fashion it using white chocolate cookies (like this one) or traditional chocolate (shown on front cover). For a completely edible version, omit the gold petal dust from the chocolate ganache "snowdrifts" and remove the dragées before serving.

CHOCOLATE COOKIE TREE

Make with a cookie tree set of 10 star-shaped cookie cutters in graduated sizes.

Cookie Tree

   White or Dark Chocolate Dreams (recipe, page 35)

Chocolate Filigree Stars

   4   ounces semisweet chocolate, divided
        and finely chopped

Chocolate Ganache

   12   ounces semisweet chocolate, finely chopped
   3/4 cup whipping cream
        Gold dragées and gold petal dust (see Note)

Prepare cookie dough as directed in recipe. For 1 large tree, cut 2 each of the 10 sizes of cookie cutters; bake 5 to 12 minutes, depending on size of cookies. For 3 small trees (as shown on cover), cut 2 each of the 5 smallest cookie cutters; bake 5 to 12 minutes, depending on size of cookies. Make a pattern for filigree stars by tracing the smallest star cookie cutter onto paper at least 3 times.(You will want to make extra stars in case any break.) Using a ruler, draw a line down center of 2 stars. Tape paper to a baking sheet; tape wax paper over paper. Temper semisweet chocolate for filigree stars (see Tempering Chocolate). Spoon tempered chocolate into a pastry bag fitted with a small round tip. Refer to photos to make 1 star and 2 star halves for each tree topper (or for a dimensional look on both sides of tree, make 1 star and 4 star halves). Pipe chocolate onto wax paper following the star outline; fill inside of outline with random lines connecting to all sides of the outline. Chill until hardened.

To make ganache, place chocolate in a heat-proof bowl. Heat whipping cream in a heavy saucepan over low heat until warm; do not boil. Pour over chocolate; stir until smooth. Allow ganache to cool until slightly thickened, about 5 minutes. (Mixture thickens as it cools; reheat over low heat, if necessary. The consistency of ganache should be similar to pudding that drops from a spoon.) Holding the largest cookie, spoon chocolate in center of cookie; drag

chocolate over each point. Place cookie on serving plate. Repeat with remaining cookies from largest to smallest, staggering points of stars and lightly pressing in place. Decorate with gold dragées and gold petal dust. Carefully peel chilled filigree stars from wax paper. Gently stand a whole star in ganache on top of tree. Arrange star halves at an angle to whole star to form a dimensional star. Allow ganache to set up.
Yield: Ganache to cover 3 small trees OR 1 large tree
Note: Gold dragées and gold petal dust are nonedible and recommended for decoration only.

TEMPERING CHOCOLATE

General Information: Tempering chocolate is a method of heating and cooling chocolate which results in a smooth texture and even color for an extended period of time. It is important to use finely chopped chocolate for tempering. Set aside one third of chocolate to add to melted chocolate for cooling. Melt remaining chocolate using double boiler method or microwave method. When chocolate is completely melted, it should register 88° to 90° for dark chocolate, 85° to 88° for milk chocolate, or 84° to 87° for white chocolate on a candy or chocolate thermometer. To test temper, wipe a thin bit of chocolate onto wax paper and chill 3 minutes. If chocolate is dry to the touch and evenly glossy, it is tempered and ready to use.
Double Boiler Method: Place remaining chocolate in double boiler and, stirring constantly, melt over hot, not simmering, water. As soon as chocolate is melted, remove from heat and add reserved chocolate. If temperature is not low enough, stir until it registers the proper temperature. If chocolate temperature drops too low, rewarm chocolate in double boiler (do not exceed 115°) and then cool to the above temperatures. Retemper as necessary.
Microwave Method: Place remaining chocolate in a microwave-safe glass bowl and microwave on medium power (50%) 1 minute; stir. Microwave 1 minute more; stir until melted. Add reserved chocolate; stir until completely melted. If temperature is not low enough, stir until it reaches the proper temperature. If chocolate temperature drops too low, rewarm chocolate in microwave and then cool until it registers the proper temperature. Retemper as necessary.

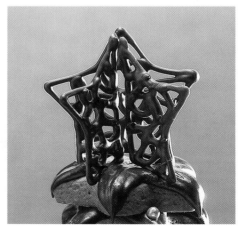

TWELFTH NIGHT
Splendor

Inspired by the gifts of the Magi, trimmings in shades of burnished gold, bronze, and copper bring the splendor of Twelfth Night to your home.

... Behold, there came Wise Men from the east to Jerusalem, saying, Where is he that is born King of the Jews? For we have seen his star in the east, and are come to worship him. ... And when they were come into the house, they saw the young child with Mary his mother, and fell down, and worshipped him: and when they had opened their treasures, they presented unto him gifts; gold, and frankincense and myrrh.

— *Matthew 2:1-2 & 11, King James Version*

Crowned with a wooden Star of Bethlehem, the richly adorned tree is a handsome focal point for the foyer. A trio of plant stands in varying heights are swathed in organza and placed among the branches to form a striking setting for resin figures of the Magi. Lengths of shimmering organza and gleaming ribbon, sparkling lights, metallic berries, and golden stars complement an elegant array of handmade trims.

Luxurious to look upon, yet oh-so-affordable to craft! Eucalyptus, Painted Glass, and Paint-Swirled Glass Ball Ornaments (*above*) are lovely additions to the evergreen — and they also make wonderful package tie-ons. The Feather Tassels and Finial Ornaments (*opposite, top*) are opulent little touches. Use your choice of stickers to create "stenciled" designs on Decorated Bottle Ornaments, then hang them on the tree or display on a side table.

Instructions for Twelfth Night Splendor begin on page 156.

Illuminate the mantel — or even a buffet — in regal style: Place tapers, votives, and pillar candles in amber glass holders and arrange among boughs of fragrant greenery. Fill in with gleaming glass balls, painted wooden stars, and glittering fruit-shaped ornaments, then tuck in sprigs of golden berries for a glorious finish.

Golden jewels, decorative wooden shapes, and metallic paints help transform humble papier-mâché containers into Elegant Boxes that are worthy of holding kingly treasures.

Even the tiniest touches can bring royal splendor to a forgotten cranny: A single Feather Tassel accents the knob of a curio cabinet with style.

To add gilded highlights to purchased resin figures, simply brush the raised areas with metallic gold or bronze paint, then use a soft cloth to wipe away excess paint while it's still wet.

Instructions for Twelfth Night Splendor *begin on page 156.*

Dress your front entrance in resplendent style: Suspend Decorated Bottle Luminaries from iron lantern hooks along the walkway to guide travelers to your home. Adorn evergreens and shrubs with oversize ornaments and create a tableau with a set of Magi figures (if you gilded your statues as described on page 58, apply a waterproof sealer before placing them outdoors). Add fullness to a lighted evergreen wreath with gold-tipped greenery picks and wrap with garlands of golden berries and gleaming ribbons, then use floral wire to attach shining trims (we selected a mixture of handmade and purchased ornaments).

Instructions for *Twelfth Night Splendor* begin on page 156.

a family affair

Christmas is truly a family affair, with celebrations encompassing two, three, or even four generations for many of us. This year, take time to appreciate the rich legacy of your holiday traditions — and create new ones for future generations.

No family gathering would be complete without wonderful things to eat! Whether your main meal is a casual buffet or a formal dinner, it's likely that there are certain dishes that everyone looks forward to year after year — perhaps Grandma's biscuits or Mom's corn pudding. Turn the page to discover new selections to add to your list of favorites.

PRALINE-MUSTARD GLAZED HAM

- 1 bone-in smoked spiral-cut ham half (7 to 8 pounds)
- 1 cup maple syrup
- 3/4 cup firmly packed light brown sugar
- 3/4 cup Dijon mustard
- 1/3 cup apple juice
- 1/4 cup raisins
- 1 cooking apple, thinly sliced

Remove skin and excess fat from smoked ham; place ham in a lightly greased 13 x 9-inch pan. Stir together maple syrup and next 3 ingredients. Pour mixture over ham. Bake at 350° on lower oven rack 2 hours and 30 minutes or until a meat thermometer inserted into thickest portion registers 140°, basting every 20 minutes with glaze. Let ham stand 10 minutes. Remove from pan, reserving drippings. If desired, cool, cover, and chill ham. Remove fat from drippings with a fat separator, and discard. Cover and chill drippings until ready to make sauce. Cook drippings, raisins, and apple slices in a saucepan over low heat 5 minutes. Serve warm sauce with ham.
Yield: 12 servings

EASY CHEDDAR BISCUITS

- 1 1/2 cups all-purpose flour
- 1 tablespoon baking powder
- 1/2 teaspoon salt
- 1 tablespoon sugar
- 1 cup (4 ounces) shredded sharp Cheddar cheese
- 1/3 cup shortening
- 1/2 cup milk

Pulse first 4 ingredients in a food processor 4 or 5 times or until dry ingredients are thoroughly combined. Add shredded cheese and shortening, and pulse 4 or 5 times or until mixture is crumbly. With processor running, gradually add milk, and process until dough forms a ball and leaves sides of bowl. Turn dough out onto a lightly floured surface; shape into a ball. Pat or roll dough to 1/2-inch thickness; cut with a 2-inch round cutter, and place on baking sheets. Bake biscuits in 2 batches at 425° for 10 minutes or until golden.
Yield: 1 1/2 dozen biscuits

This bountiful spread features a heavenly Praline-Mustard Glazed Ham, elegant **Green Beans Amandine,** fiery Cajun Black-Eyed Peas, **Easy Cheddar Biscuits,** and a hearty Corn Pudding. (*Right*) Delectably spicy **Hot Curried Fruit** can also double as a dessert topping.

HOT CURRIED FRUIT

- 1 can (29 ounces) pear halves, drained
- 1 can (29 ounces) peach halves, drained
- 1 can (20 ounces) pineapple chunks, drained
- 2 cans (15 1/4 ounces each) apricot halves, drained
- 1/2 cup butter or margarine, softened
- 1 cup firmly packed brown sugar
- 1 tablespoon cornstarch
- 1 1/2 teaspoons curry powder

Place first 4 ingredients in a 13 x 9-inch baking dish. Combine butter and remaining 3 ingredients; spoon over fruit. Bake at 325° for 1 hour, basting occasionally with cooking liquid. Serve with a slotted spoon.
Yield: 8 to 10 servings
Note: You can prepare casserole ahead and store it in the refrigerator up to 2 days; bake according to directions just before serving.

GREEN BEANS AMANDINE

- 1/2 cup sliced almonds
- 2 pounds fresh green beans
- 1/3 cup butter or margarine
- 1 tablespoon lemon juice
- 1 teaspoon salt
- 1/4 teaspoon pepper

Bake sliced almonds in a shallow pan at 350° for 5 to 10 minutes or until toasted. Set almonds aside. Split beans lengthwise. Cook beans in boiling water to cover in a Dutch oven 4 minutes or until tender; drain. Melt butter in Dutch oven; add almonds, beans, lemon juice, salt, and pepper, tossing to coat. Serve immediately.
Yield: 10 servings

Cajun Black-Eyed Peas

- 1 pound dried black-eyed peas
- 8 cups water
- 6 slices bacon
- 1 bunch green onions, chopped
- 1 large onion, chopped
- 1 green bell pepper, chopped
- 1 cup chopped fresh parsley
- 1 small jalapeño pepper, seeded and minced
- 3 cloves garlic, pressed
- 2 tablespoons Worcestershire sauce
- 1/4 teaspoon hot sauce
- 1 1/2 teaspoons salt
- 1 teaspoon pepper
- 1/4 teaspoon dried oregano
- 1/4 teaspoon dried thyme
- 1 pound smoked sausage, sliced
- 1 1/2 cups chopped smoked ham (about 1/2 pound)
- 1 can (14 1/2 ounces) diced tomatoes with green pepper, celery, and onion, undrained

Sort and wash peas; place in a large Dutch oven, and add water to a depth of 2 inches above peas. Cover and let stand 8 hours or overnight.

Drain peas, and return to Dutch oven. Add 8 cups water; bring to a boil. Cover, reduce heat, and simmer 30 minutes, stirring occasionally. Add bacon and next 12 ingredients; return to a boil. Cover, reduce heat, and simmer 30 minutes or until black-eyed peas are tender. Add sausage, ham, and tomatoes; return to a boil. Cover, reduce heat, and simmer 30 minutes. Remove bacon, if desired.

Yield: 14 servings

Corn Pudding

- 4 cans (15 1/4 ounces each) whole kernel corn, drained and divided
- 1/2 cup all-purpose flour
- 1/3 cup sugar
- 6 tablespoons butter or margarine, melted
- 2 tablespoons cornmeal
- 1 1/2 cups milk
- 4 large eggs
- 1/2 teaspoon salt

Process 1 can corn, flour, and next 6 ingredients in a blender or food processor until smooth, stopping to scrape down sides. Transfer to a bowl; stir in remaining 3 cans of corn. Pour mixture into a lightly greased 8-inch square baking dish. Bake at 350° for 35 minutes or until set.

Yield: 12 servings

Note: When baking in a 2-quart casserole, allow 1 hour baking time or until set.

Oven "Fried" Chicken Fingers with Honey-Mustard Dipping Sauce

Sauce
- 1/4 cup honey
- 1/4 cup spicy brown mustard

Chicken
- 1 1/2 pounds chicken breast tenders (about 16 pieces)
- 1/2 cup low-fat buttermilk
- 1/2 cup coarsely crushed cornflakes
- 1/4 cup seasoned breadcrumbs
- 1 tablespoon instant minced onion
- 1 teaspoon paprika
- 1/4 teaspoon dried thyme
- 1/4 teaspoon black pepper
- 1 tablespoon vegetable oil

To prepare sauce, combine honey and mustard in a small bowl; cover and chill. Preheat oven to 400°. To prepare chicken, combine chicken and buttermilk in a shallow dish; cover and chill 15 minutes. Drain chicken, discarding liquid. Combine cornflakes and next 5 ingredients (cornflakes through pepper) in a large zip-top plastic bag; add 4 chicken pieces to bag. Seal and shake to coat. Repeat procedure with remaining chicken. Spread oil evenly in a jellyroll pan, and arrange chicken in a single layer in pan. Bake at 400° for 4 minutes on each side or until done. Serve with sauce.

Yield: 8 servings (serving size: 2 chicken tenders and 1 tablespoon sauce)

Quick Gingerbread Cookies

- 1 package (18 ounces) refrigerated sugar cookie dough
- 2 teaspoons molasses
- 1/4 to 1/2 cup all-purpose flour, divided
- 1 tablespoon ground cinnamon
- 1/8 teaspoon ground ginger
- 1 to 2 teaspoons cocoa (optional)
  Purchased frosting and candies

Preheat oven to 350°. Flatten dough on a lightly floured surface. Drizzle molasses over dough. Sprinkle 1/4 cup flour, cinnamon, and ginger over dough. For a darker dough, add cocoa with dry ingredients. Knead ingredients into dough until well blended, using additional flour as necessary. On a lightly floured surface, use a floured rolling pin to roll out dough to 1/4-inch thickness. Use a cookie cutter to cut out dough. Transfer to a greased baking sheet. Bake 6 to 8 minutes or until bottoms are lightly browned. Transfer cookies to a wire rack to cool. Decorate with frosting and candies.

Yield: about 1 dozen cookies

Why not indulge the children with a special "kids-only" menu? Include good-for-you treats that will tempt young appetites: Oven "Fried" Chicken Fingers to dunk in sweet Honey-Mustard Dipping Sauce, Quick-and-Easy Macaroni and Cheese, and Rudolph's Apple Salad.

QUICK-AND-EASY MACARONI AND CHEESE

- 8 ounces large elbow macaroni, cooked
- 1 package (8 ounces) shredded sharp Cheddar cheese
- 1 can (10³/₄ ounces) cream of mushroom soup, undiluted
- ¹/₂ cup mayonnaise
- ¹/₂ cup milk

Stir together all ingredients in a lightly greased 2¹/₂-quart baking dish. Bake at 375° for 25 minutes.
Yield: 6 servings
Note: Reduced-fat sharp Cheddar cheese, reduced-fat cream of mushroom soup, light mayonnaise, and fat-free milk may be substituted.

RUDOLPH'S APPLE SALAD

To serve as a dessert, spoon into waffle ice-cream bowls.

- 2 large Red Delicious apples, coarsely chopped
- 1 large Granny Smith apple, coarsely chopped
- 1 celery rib, diced
- 1¹/₂ cups miniature marshmallows
- ¹/₄ cup mayonnaise
- ¹/₂ cup lemon yogurt
- 2 cups granola

Stir together chopped apples and next 4 ingredients. Spoon mixture evenly into 8 individual serving dishes. Sprinkle with granola just before serving.
Yield: 8 servings

POPCORN DELIGHT

- 8 cups popped popcorn
- 3 cups corn chips, coarsely crushed
- 2 cups crispy corn puffs cereal
- 1 pound white chocolate, chopped
- 2 cups candy-coated chocolate pieces
     (optional)

Combine first 3 ingredients in a large bowl. Microwave white chocolate in a glass bowl at HIGH power 2 to 3 minutes, stirring every minute, until chocolate melts. Drizzle over popcorn mixture, tossing to coat. Stir in candy-coated chocolate pieces, if desired. Spread in a wax paper-lined 15 x 10-inch jellyroll pan; chill 30 minutes. Break into pieces; store in an airtight container.

Yield: 15 cups

While the grownups are visiting or preparing dinner, keep the kids occupied with a crafty activity area. They'll have a blast coloring Reindeer Placemats or making festive **Photo Ornaments.** Don't forget to provide plenty of munchies — we made a big batch of Popcorn Delight.

Instructions for A Family Affair are on page 158.

Making Memories

Preserve holiday memories for a lifetime. Stock up on film, batteries, and tapes for your cameras and video recorders and capture the day's events on film.

Get out the old family photo albums — the younger folks will enjoy seeing snapshots from their parents' childhood. Ask Grandmother and Grandfather what Christmas was like when they were growing up.

Take pictures of the everyday joys of the season: everyone trimming the tree, the kids wrapping presents, Mom baking cookies, the children just waking up, etc.

Let the children display their artwork for everyone to see — hang **Miniature Hand Ornaments** (*above*) on the tree, or use them to dress up wrapped packages. "**Handy**" **Gift Tags** (*right*) are fun and easy to decorate with glitter, pom-poms, and other fancies.

Along with the candid shots, be sure to take several photographs of the entire family to add to next year's scrapbook. Get pictures of the kids at play, too. If your gathering is on Christmas Eve, let them decorate **Quick Gingerbread Cookies** to leave out for Santa.

Instructions for A Family Affair are on page 158.

PECAN PIE COOKIES

1¼ cups butter or margarine, softened and divided
½ cup sugar
½ cup plus 3 tablespoons dark corn syrup, divided
2 large eggs, separated
2½ cups all-purpose flour
½ cup powdered sugar
¾ cup finely chopped pecans

Beat 1 cup butter and sugar at medium speed with an electric mixer until light and fluffy. Add ½ cup corn syrup and egg yolks, beating well. Gradually stir in flour; cover and chill 1 hour. Melt ¼ cup butter in a heavy saucepan over medium heat; stir in powdered sugar and 3 tablespoons corn syrup. Cook, stirring often, until mixture boils. Remove from heat. Stir in pecans; chill 30 minutes.

Shape mixture by ½ teaspoonfuls into ¼-inch balls; set aside. Shape cookie dough into 1-inch balls; place 2 inches apart on ungreased baking sheets. Beat egg whites until foamy; brush on dough balls. Bake at 375° for 6 minutes. Remove from oven, and place pecan balls in center of each cookie. Bake 6 to 8 more minutes or until lightly browned. Cool 5 minutes on baking pans; remove to wire racks to cool completely. Freeze up to 1 month, if desired.
Yield: 4½ dozen cookies

CRACKED CARAMEL-PUMPKIN PIE

½ package (15 ounces) refrigerated piecrusts
1 can (14 ounces) sweetened condensed milk
1 can (15 ounces) pumpkin
2 cups whipping cream, divided
2 large eggs, lightly beaten
2 egg yolks, lightly beaten
¼ cup firmly packed brown sugar
½ teaspoon pumpkin pie spice
3 tablespoons water
3 tablespoons corn syrup
⅓ cup sugar

Fit piecrust into a 9-inch pieplate; fold edges under, and crimp. Cook milk in a medium-size heavy saucepan over medium-high heat, whisking constantly, 10 minutes or until thickened and bubbly. Remove from heat; stir in pumpkin. Stir in 1 cup whipping cream and next 4 ingredients until smooth. Pour into crust. Bake at 350° on bottom oven rack for 40 minutes. Cool on a wire rack. Chill 8 hours.

Cook 3 tablespoons water, corn syrup, and sugar in a small saucepan over medium heat, without stirring, until a candy thermometer registers 300° (hard-crack stage). Pour immediately over pie, and quickly spread mixture with a metal spatula. Let stand 2 hours before serving. Tap hard sugar topping with back of a spoon to crack. Beat remaining 1 cup whipping cream at medium speed with an electric mixer until soft peaks form. Serve with pie.
Yield: 1 (9-inch) pie

GRANDMA'S CHOCOLATE CAKE

2 cups all-purpose flour
2 cups sugar
¼ cup cocoa
1 teaspoon ground cinnamon
1 cup butter or margarine
1 cup water
1 teaspoon baking soda
2 large eggs
½ cup buttermilk
1 teaspoon vanilla extract
1 package (12 ounces) small chocolate-covered peppermint patties, unwrapped
  Chocolate Frosting

Combine first 4 ingredients, and set aside. Combine butter and water in a large saucepan; bring to a boil. Remove from heat; stir in soda. Add flour mixture, stirring well. Stir in eggs, buttermilk, and vanilla. Spoon batter into a greased and floured 13 x 9-inch pan. Bake at 350° for 30 minutes. Top with candy; bake 2 additional minutes or until candy softens enough to spread. Gently spread melted candy over warm cake. Spread Chocolate Frosting over top. Cut into squares.
Yield: 15 servings

CHOCOLATE FROSTING

½ cup butter or margarine
⅓ cup milk
1 package (16 ounces) powdered sugar, sifted
¼ cup cocoa
1 teaspoon vanilla extract

Combine butter and milk in large saucepan. Bring mixture to a boil, and remove from heat. Combine powdered sugar and cocoa; add to butter mixture. Add vanilla, stirring until smooth.
Yield: 2 cups frosting

WARM CITRUS CIDER

1 orange
1 lemon
1 teaspoon whole cloves
2 quarts apple cider
  Cinnamon sticks (optional)

Cut long strips of orange and lemon rind, reserving fruit for other uses. Insert cloves into rind strips. Cook rind strips and cider in a Dutch oven over medium heat 5 minutes or until thoroughly heated (do not boil). Serve with cinnamon sticks, if desired.
Yield: 2 quarts cider

Everyone knows that dessert is the best part of any meal! Here's a smorgasbord of treats to add to your menu: **Grandma's Chocolate Cake** topped with Chocolate Frosting and mints, tempting **Pecan Pie Cookies**, and crispy-creamy Cracked Caramel-Pumpkin Pie. Serve cups of **Warm Citrus Cider** with cinnamon sticks and clove-studded lemon twists.

the Sharing

# of CHRISTMAS

As we celebrate the arrival of God's greatest gift, it's only natural that we in turn share that spirit with family and friends. We make it easy with handcrafted notions, tasty treats from your kitchen, and creative packaging. Need lots of gifts for teachers or co-workers? No problem — we've got plenty of time- and money-saving ideas for making several gifts at once!

Dress up a gift of wine or sparkling cider with a festive Bottle Sleeve and Tag. What an easy, inexpensive way to make an ordinary gift extra special!

Merry Christmas

Crafty Creations *to* Share

We all enjoy receiving handcrafted gifts, but who has the time to make them? You do! You'll find lots of nifty ideas for heartfelt gifts and winning wrappings on the following pages — and the best part is that you can easily make several of each to share with all your friends.

Who wouldn't love to open a Christmas card and discover a hand-painted **Charm Pin** to wear on her favorite blouse? Craft and hobby shops offer a wide variety of decorative metal charms, from whimsical to romantic. Use your imagination to add painted embellishments, then glue on a pin back and attach to a handmade **Greeting Card**.

Instructions for Crafty Creations to Share *begin on page 159.*

To make little gifts unforgettable, present them in festively trimmed **Gift Boxes** and attach eye-catching **Tag Ornaments**. You can wrap up tiny treats for your friends at the office or church, and all of your children's teachers!

Instructions for Crafty Creations to Share begin on page 159.

It's easy (and inexpensive) to treat your friends to a little bit of luxury with these Bottled Bath Salts. Simply purchase a bulk package of bath salts, pour into several small bottles, decorate, and voilà! … you've got lots of wonderful gifts. For an added touch of elegance, tie on sparkling Gift Tags.

For extra-special friends and family members, create naturally elegant Handmade Soaps! Make as many different varieties as you like — you can customize the ingredients and fragrances to suit the recipients' tastes. You'll find a selection of colors and scents among the soapmaking supplies at your local craft store. Embellish wrapped bars with lengths of crimped paper and shimmering ribbon; present in the gift boxes or baskets of your choice.

Floral alphabet stickers make it easy to personalize pretty **Rose Petal Sachets**. Monogram single potpourri bags for all your friends, or fill a basket for someone who enjoys feminine fancies.

Share the light of the season with these tiny Flowerpot Candles — they're simple to make and decorate with beaded dangles! You can choose colors and trims to suit your friends' personalities: try animal prints for the adventuresome or lace for the romantic.

Instructions for Crafty Creations to Share begin on page 159.

Filled with foil-wrapped chocolates, blossoming Flowerpot Favors are delicious delights for a holiday "girls' night out." If you prefer a wintry look, exchange the pastel blooms and bows for vivid poinsettias and crimson ribbon … the gold-leafed pots are so versatile!

Instructions for Crafty Creations to Share begin on page 159.

Why settle for ordinary, mass-produced wrapping paper for your presents when you can design your own Custom Gift Bags using plain white lunch sacks and fanciful print tissue paper? You can even craft coordinating gift tags — just cut motifs from the tissue paper and glue onto card stock! Colorful coated craft wire and buttons make fun finishing touches.

Gourmet GIFTS
from Your Kitchen

You don't have to spend a fortune at a gourmet shop for deliciously unique gifts! With a little bit of kitchen know-how and our creative recipes and packaging ideas, it's easy and inexpensive. Whether you need one large gift for a family or lots of little goodies for co-workers, you'll find the perfect treat. Turn the page and get a head start on the holidays!

On the following pages, you'll find tempting confections, helpful mixes, and a variety of baked goods to please everyone on your gift list … and most are made using items you probably already have in your kitchen. Feel free to mix and match our packaging ideas for one-of-a-kind presentations!

COCONUT SWIRLS

- $1/3$ cup butter or margarine
- 3 tablespoons water
- 1 teaspoon vanilla extract
- 2 cups sifted powdered sugar
- $1/2$ cup instant nonfat dry milk powder
- 3 cups flaked coconut
- 4 ounces chocolate candy coating, melted

Melt butter in a medium saucepan over low heat. Remove from heat, and stir in water and vanilla. Combine powdered sugar and milk powder; stir $1/2$ cup at a time into butter mixture until smooth. Stir in coconut. Shape into 1-inch balls, and place on ungreased baking sheets. Chill 20 minutes. Spoon melted candy coating into a small heavy-duty zip-top plastic bag; seal. Snip a tiny hole in 1 corner of bag, and drizzle coating over coconut balls.
Yield: 3 dozen candies

DOUBLE-NUT BUTTERSCOTCH FUDGE

- 1 package (11 ounces) butterscotch morsels
- 1 can (14 ounces) sweetened condensed milk
- $1^1/2$ cups miniature marshmallows
- $2/3$ cup chunky peanut butter
- 1 teaspoon vanilla extract
- $1/8$ teaspoon salt
- 1 cup chopped pecans

Cook first 3 ingredients in a large heavy saucepan over medium heat, stirring constantly, 5 to 6 minutes or until smooth; remove from heat. Stir in peanut butter, vanilla, and salt until blended; stir in pecans. Pour into a buttered 9-inch square pan. Chill until firm; cut into squares. Store fudge in refrigerator.
Yield: $2^1/2$ pounds fudge
Note: For ease, microwave first 3 ingredients in a 2-quart microwave-safe bowl at HIGH power 2 to 3 minutes or until melted, stirring twice.

DATE BALLS

- $1/2$ cup butter or margarine, softened
- 1 cup sugar
- 1 package (10 ounces) chopped dates
- 1 large egg, lightly beaten
- 1 cup chopped pecans, toasted
- 1 teaspoon vanilla extract
- 4 cups crisp rice cereal
  Powdered sugar

Combine first 4 ingredients in a saucepan; cook over low heat 6 to 8 minutes, stirring constantly, until sugar dissolves. Add pecans, and cook, stirring constantly, 10 minutes. Remove from heat, and stir in vanilla. Stir in cereal, and cool slightly. Shape mixture into $1^1/2$-inch balls; roll in powdered sugar.
Yield: $3^1/2$ dozen candies

CHERRY-PISTACHIO BARK

- $1^1/4$ cups dried cherries
- 2 tablespoons water
- 2 packages (12 ounces each) white chocolate morsels
- 12 ounces vanilla candy coating
- $1^1/4$ cups chopped red or green pistachios

Microwave cherries and water in a small glass bowl at HIGH power 2 minutes; drain. Melt chocolate and candy coating in a heavy saucepan over low heat. Remove from heat, and stir in cherries and pistachios. Spread into a wax paper-lined 15 x 10-inch jellyroll pan. Chill 1 hour or until firm. Break into pieces.
Yield: about 3 pounds candy

No one can resist the appeal of homemade candy, especially when it's as scrumptious as easy-to-make Date Balls, Cherry-Pistachio Bark, Double-Nut Butterscotch Fudge, and Coconut Swirls! For thoughtful little gifts, deliver them in fancy Decorated Candy Boxes.

Instructions for Gourmet Gifts from Your Kitchen begin on page 163.

BLOND BROWNIE MIX

- 1 1/8 cups firmly packed light brown sugar
- 1 cup self-rising flour
- 3/4 cup chopped pecans
- 3/4 cup flaked coconut
- 1/2 cup golden raisins

Layer ingredients in an airtight container. Store in a cool, dry place up to 2 months.

Yield: makes about 4 cups mix

To Bake: Beat 2 large eggs, 1/4 cup softened butter, and 1 1/2 teaspoons vanilla extract at medium speed with an electric mixer; gradually add mix, beating until blended. Spoon into a greased and floured 8-inch square pan. Bake at 350° for 20 minutes; reduce temperature to 325°, and bake 25 more minutes. Cool in pan on a wire rack. Cut into squares.

Yield: 16 brownies

Note: Use a 9-inch square pan for a smaller brownie. After reducing temperature to 325°, bake for 20 minutes. Makes 25 brownies.

Mixes make great gifts! We packed all of ours in **Decorated Clay Pots** and **Tin Containers**. Share a batch of **Blond Brownies** along with a bag of mix and instructions for baking more. Our **Cajun Seasoning Blend** will spice up the season for a favorite cook — deliver it in a painted pot with a zesty chile pepper tag.

CAJUN SEASONING BLEND

Use smaller decorated pots to make several gifts.

- 2 tablespoons dried basil
- 2 tablespoons crushed black peppercorns
- 1 tablespoon ground white pepper
- 1 tablespoon cumin seeds, crushed
- 1 tablespoon caraway seeds, crushed
- 1 tablespoon fennel seeds, crushed
- 1 tablespoon dried thyme
- 1 tablespoon dried oregano
- 1 1/2 teaspoons salt
- 1 1/2 teaspoons dried crushed red pepper
- 2 tablespoons paprika

Combine first 10 ingredients in a small skillet. Cook over medium-high heat 3 minutes or until seeds are lightly browned. Remove from heat; stir in paprika. Store in an airtight container; shake well before each use. Use to coat chicken, beef, pork, or fish, or sprinkle over grilled corn or baked potatoes.

Yield: 3/4 cup mix

MEXICAN MOCHA MIX

- 1 cup cocoa
- 1 cup sugar
- $^1/_2$ cup powdered nondairy coffee creamer
- 2 tablespoons instant coffee granules
- 1 teaspoon ground cinnamon
- $^1/_2$ teaspoon ground nutmeg

Combine all ingredients in a large heavy-duty zip-top plastic bag; seal and shake to blend. Spoon $^1/_4$ cup mixture into coffee mug, and stir in 1 cup hot water.
Yield: 10 servings

Cinnamon lends distinctive flavor to Mexican Mocha Mix. We trimmed a painted pot with silvery ribbon and glued shiny cup-and-saucer charms to the gift tag.

Instructions for Gourmet Gifts from Your Kitchen *begin on page 163.*

Instructions for Gourmet Gifts from Your Kitchen *begin on page 163.*

SEASONED RICE MIX

- 3 cups uncooked long-grain rice
- $^1/_4$ cup dried parsley flakes
- 2 tablespoons chicken bouillon granules
- 2 teaspoons onion powder
- $^1/_2$ teaspoon garlic powder
- $^1/_4$ teaspoon dried thyme

Stir together all ingredients. Place 1 cup mixture into each of 3 airtight containers. Store in a cool, dry place.
Yield: 3 cups mix
To Serve: Bring 2 cups water and 1 tablespoon butter or margarine to a boil in a saucepan; stir in 1 cup rice mix. Cover, reduce heat, and simmer 20 minutes or until liquid is absorbed.
Yield: 4 servings

Busy moms will enjoy Seasoned Rice Mix — and one batch makes enough for three gifts! Tuck the mix and cooking directions in paper-covered or bead-embellished tins.

Holiday munchers will love savory Cheddar Cheese Loaf, as well as flavorful Orange Blossom Muffins, Miniature Cinnamon Loaves, and Mini Apricot-Pecan Loaves. Experiment with different shapes — adjust baking time to make loaves and regular or mini muffins using any of these recipes (see page 164 for pan sizes). Try our easy-to-decorate Mini-Loaf Bag, Mini-Muffin Box, or Painted Clay Plate to package smaller items; or an eye-catching Loaf Wrapper for a full-size portion.

Instructions for Gourmet Gifts from Your Kitchen begin on page 163.

MINIATURE CINNAMON LOAVES

    1   package (18.25 ounces) yellow cake mix with
          pudding
    4   large eggs
  3/4   cup vegetable oil
  3/4   cup water
    1   teaspoon vanilla extract
  1/2   cup sugar
    3   tablespoons ground cinnamon

Beat first 5 ingredients at high speed with an electric mixer 3 minutes. Combine sugar and cinnamon. Pour half of batter evenly into 5 greased and floured 5 3/4 x 3 1/4 x 2-inch disposable loafpans. Sprinkle evenly with half of sugar mixture. Pour remaining batter into pans. Sprinkle with remaining sugar mixture; gently swirl with a knife. Bake at 350° for 35 minutes or until a wooden pick inserted in center comes out clean. Cool in pans on wire racks. Store in freezer, if desired.

For larger Cinnamon Loaves: Pour half of batter evenly into 2 greased and floured 8 x 3 3/4-inch disposable loafpans. Stir together sugar and cinnamon; sprinkle half of sugar mixture evenly over batter in loafpans. Pour remaining batter evenly into loafpans. Sprinkle with remaining sugar mixture; gently swirl with a knife. Bake at 350° for 45 minutes or until a wooden pick inserted in center comes out clean.

Yield: 5 small or 2 large loaves

ORANGE BLOSSOM MUFFINS

    2   cups biscuit mix
  1/4   cup sugar
    1   large egg, lightly beaten
  1/2   cup orange juice
    2   tablespoons vegetable oil
  1/2   cup orange marmalade
  1/2   cup chopped pecans
    3   tablespoons sugar
    1   tablespoon all-purpose flour
  1/2   teaspoon ground cinnamon
  1/4   teaspoon ground nutmeg

Combine biscuit mix and 1/4 cup sugar in a large bowl; make a well in center of mixture. Combine egg, orange juice, and oil; add to biscuit mixture, stirring just until moistened. Stir in marmalade and pecans. Place paper baking cups in miniature (1 3/4-inch) muffin pans; spoon 1 tablespoon batter into each cup. Combine 3 tablespoons sugar and next 3 ingredients; sprinkle over muffins. Bake at 400° for 10 to 12 minutes or until lightly browned. Cool in pans on wire racks.

Yield: 3 1/2 dozen mini muffins

CHEDDAR CHEESE LOAF

  3 3/4   cups biscuit mix
    3/4   cup shredded sharp Cheddar cheese
  1 1/2   cups milk
      1   egg
    1/8   to 1/4 teaspoon ground red pepper

Combine biscuit mix and cheese. Add milk, egg, and pepper, stirring 2 minutes or until blended. Spoon into a greased 9 x 5-inch loafpan. Bake loaf at 350° for 45 minutes. Cool on wire rack.

Yield: 1 loaf

MINI APRICOT-PECAN LOAVES

This bread is great for Christmas giving.

  2 1/2   cups dried apricots, chopped
      1   cup chopped pecans
      4   cups all-purpose flour, divided
    1/4   cup butter or margarine, softened
      2   cups sugar
      2   large eggs
      1   tablespoon plus 1 teaspoon baking powder
    1/2   teaspoon baking soda
    1/2   teaspoon salt
  1 1/2   cups orange juice

Cover apricots with warm water in a large bowl; let stand 30 minutes. Drain apricots. Stir in pecans and 1/2 cup flour; set aside. Beat butter at medium speed with an electric mixer 2 minutes; gradually add sugar, beating well. Add eggs, 1 at a time, beating after each addition. Combine remaining 3 1/2 cups flour, baking powder, soda, and salt. Add to butter mixture alternately with orange juice, beginning and ending with flour mixture. Stir in apricot mixture. Spoon into 5 greased and floured 5 3/4 x 3 1/4 x 2-inch disposable loafpans; let stand at room temperature 20 minutes.

Bake at 350° for 50 minutes or until a wooden pick inserted in center comes out clean. Cool in pans on wire rack.

Yield: 5 loaves

CHOCOLATE PINWHEEL LOAF

These pretty spiraled loaves are easy to make. Just stir melted chocolate into half the dough; then roll the doughs together, jellyroll fashion.

- 1/2 cup milk
- 1/4 cup butter or margarine
- 1/4 cup sugar
- 3/4 teaspoon salt
- 1 package active dry yeast
- 1/4 cup warm water (105° to 115°)
- 2 large eggs, beaten
- 3 to 3 1/4 cups all-purpose flour
- 1 square (1 ounce) unsweetened chocolate, melted and cooled
  Glaze

Combine first 4 ingredients in a saucepan; heat until butter melts. Remove from heat, and cool to 105° to 115°. Combine yeast and warm water in a 1-cup liquid measuring cup; let stand 5 minutes. Combine yeast mixture, liquid mixture, eggs, and 2 cups flour in a large mixing bowl; beat at medium speed with an electric mixer until smooth. Transfer half of mixture to a second bowl. Beat melted chocolate into one portion of mixture. Stir enough remaining flour into each portion to make a soft dough. Knead each portion of dough on a floured surface until smooth and elastic (8 to 10 minutes). Place each in a well-greased bowl, turning to grease top. Cover and let rise in a warm place (85°), free from drafts, 45 minutes or until doubled in bulk.

Punch each dough down, and turn out onto a floured surface; roll each into an 18 x 10-inch rectangle. Position chocolate dough on top of plain dough. Cut dough in half to make two 10 x 9-inch pieces. Roll each piece, jellyroll fashion, starting at short end. Pinch seams and ends together; fold ends under. Place, seam-side down, in 2 greased 8 1/2 x 4 1/2-inch loafpans. Cover and let rise in a warm place, free from drafts, 45 minutes or until doubled in bulk.

Bake at 350° for 20 minutes or until loaves are golden. Remove from pan; place on a wire rack. Drizzle Glaze over warm loaf. Serve warm or cool.
Yield: 2 loaves

GLAZE

- 1 cup sifted powdered sugar
- 1 1/2 tablespoons milk
- 1/2 teaspoon vanilla extract

Combine all ingredients, stirring well.
Yield: about 1/3 cup glaze

PECAN MINI-MUFFINS

These muffins taste like pecan tassies but are easier to prepare because there's no separate crust.

- 1 cup firmly packed brown sugar
- 1/2 cup butter or margarine, melted
- 2 large eggs
- 1 teaspoon vanilla extract
- 1 cup chopped pecans
- 1/2 cup all-purpose flour

Combine first 4 ingredients in a bowl, beating with a wire whisk until smooth. Stir in pecans and flour. Place paper baking cups in miniature (1 3/4-inch) muffin pans, spoon 1 tablespoon batter into each cup. Bake at 375° for 12 minutes or until lightly browned. Cool in pans on wire racks.
Yield: 3 dozen mini muffins

WHITE CHOCOLATE-MACADAMIA NUT MUFFINS

- 2 1/2 cups biscuit mix
- 1/2 cup sugar
- 3/4 cup coarsely chopped white chocolate
- 1/2 cup coarsely chopped macadamia nuts
- 3/4 cup half-and-half
- 3 tablespoons vegetable oil
- 2 teaspoons vanilla extract
- 1 large egg, lightly beaten

Combine biscuit mix and sugar in a large bowl; stir in chocolate and nuts. Make a well in center of mixture. Combine half-and-half and remaining 3 ingredients; add to dry ingredients, stirring just until dry ingredients are moistened. Spoon into 6 (3 1/2 x 1 3/4-inch) greased muffin pans, filling two-thirds full. Bake at 400° for 15 to 18 minutes or until a wooden pick inserted into center comes out clean. Remove from pans immediately.
Yield: 1/2 dozen muffins

Cozy red-checked fabric adds country style to these baked goods! Slide a Chocolate Pinwheel Loaf into a simple fabric or embellished paper Loaf Bag, or package yummy Pecan Mini-Muffins in a charming Muffin Bag. For a teatime treat, tuck gourmet tea bags and an oversize White Chocolate-Macadamia Nut Muffin in a Painted Mug.

Instructions for Gourmet Gifts from Your Kitchen begin on page 163.

BUTTERMILK POUND CAKE

Buttermilk lends a tangy bonus to this homey cake.

- ½ cup butter or margarine, softened
- ½ cup shortening
- 2 cups sugar
- 4 large eggs
- ½ teaspoon baking soda
- 1 cup buttermilk
- 3 cups all-purpose flour
- ⅛ teaspoon salt
- 2 teaspoons lemon extract
- 1 teaspoon almond extract
- Glaze (recipe, page 92)

Beat butter and shortening at medium speed with an electric mixer 2 minutes or until creamy. Gradually add sugar, beating 5 to 7 minutes. Add eggs, one at a time, beating just until yellow disappears. Dissolve soda in buttermilk. Combine flour and salt; add to butter mixture alternately with buttermilk, beginning and ending with flour mixture. Mix at low speed after each addition just until blended. Stir in flavorings. Pour batter into a greased and floured 10-inch tube pan. Bake at 350° for 1 hour or until a wooden pick inserted in center comes out clean. Cool in pan on a wire rack 10 to 15 minutes; remove from pan, and cool completely on wire rack. Spoon Glaze over cake.

Yield: 14 servings

Note: Cake may also be baked at 350° in two 9 x 5-inch loafpans for 45 to 50 minutes or in miniature tube pans for 30 minutes.

Chocolate Swirl Pound Cake: Melt 1 tablespoon shortening and 1 square (1 ounce) unsweetened chocolate in a saucepan, stirring until smooth. Set aside. Prepare batter for Buttermilk Pound Cake, using vanilla extract in place of lemon extract. Remove 2 cups of batter; add chocolate mixture to batter, stirring until blended. Spoon one-third of remaining plain batter into a greased and floured 10-inch tube pan; top with half of chocolate batter. Repeat layers, ending with plain batter. Swirl batter with a knife to create marbled effect. Bake as directed above.

Raspberry Swirl Pound Cake: Prepare batter for Buttermilk Pound Cake. Remove 2 cups of batter; add ¼ cup melted seedless raspberry jam, stirring until blended. Spoon half of plain batter into a greased and floured 10-inch tube pan; top with raspberry batter, then remaining plain batter. Swirl batter with a knife to create marbled effect. Bake as directed above.

Send wishes for a happy holiday with this whimsical Painted Snowman Plate and a generous helping of rich Buttermilk Pound Cake swirled with chocolate or raspberry. You can also bake mini cakes to share — how fun!

Instructions for Gourmet Gifts from Your Kitchen begin on page 163.

the Tastes

# of CHRISTMAS

Family dinners, festive fêtes, classroom parties, casual get-togethers, office potlucks … it seems that every occasion calls for food during the holidays! (And let's not forget weekday dinners.) Whether you're looking for a full-scale meal or some exciting new dishes to jazz up your standard menu, you'll find the perfect solution to any dining dilemma on the following pages.

Fast Food

Between decking the halls and hitting the mall, there's hardly any time to make meals for your family (not to mention holiday guests). You need good food … FAST! Take a look at these quick-to-fix recipes. We've got you covered, from main dishes to sides, snacks, and desserts.

Oh, so good — and oh, so easy to make: Serve a tangy Black Pepper-Chèvre Cheese Log with toasted baguette slices, or set out a bowl of Quick Fiesta Dip for snacking. Need a veggie to dress up dinner? Try one of our Speedy Sides, like colorful asparagus and tomatoes drizzled with dressing. *(Right)* Top wedges of Brownie-Mint Pie with ice cream and fudge sauce for a yummy treat.

BLACK PEPPER-CHÈVRE CHEESE LOG

- 2 tablespoons cracked black pepper
- 1 Chèvre cheese log (11 ounces)
- 2 tablespoons extra virgin olive oil
  Garnish: fresh rosemary sprigs
  Toasted baguette slices

Sprinkle pepper on a square of wax paper. Roll cheese log over pepper to coat. Drizzle with olive oil. Garnish, if desired. Serve with toasted baguette slices.
Yield: 6 to 8 appetizer servings
Prep: 5 minutes

QUICK FIESTA DIP

- 1 package (9 ounces) frozen corn niblets
- 1 jar (12 ounces) thick-and-chunky mild salsa
- 1 cup (4 ounces) shredded Colby or Cheddar cheese
  Tortilla chips or corn chips

Cook corn according to package directions; drain. Pour salsa into a 9-inch glass pieplate or a bowl; stir in corn. Cover with plastic wrap; fold back a small section of wrap to allow steam to escape. Microwave at HIGH power 2 minutes or until bubbly. Sprinkle cheese over salsa; cover with plastic wrap. Let stand 5 minutes or until cheese is melted. Serve with chips.
Yield: 1 1/2 cups dip
Prep: 5 minutes, **Cook:** 7 minutes

BROWNIE-MINT PIE

For a different garnish, use a vegetable peeler to shave mints for chocolate curls.

- 1 package (4.6 ounces) chocolate mints
- 1 package (15.8 ounces) brownie mix
- 1 unbaked (9-inch) deep-dish frozen pastry shell
  Vanilla ice cream
  Hot fudge topping

Chop chocolate mints; set aside 3 tablespoons. Prepare brownie mix according to package directions, stirring remaining chopped mints into brownie batter. Pour into pastry shell. Bake at 350° for 45 minutes or until done; cool slightly. Serve with ice cream, hot fudge topping, and 3 tablespoons chopped mints.
Yield: 1 (9-inch) pie
Prep: 10 minutes, **Bake:** 45 minutes

CHUNKY CHEESE SOUP

- 2 cups frozen hash browns
- 2 cans (14 1/2 ounces each) chicken broth
- 1/2 package (16 ounces) frozen mixed vegetables
- 1 small onion, chopped
- 1/8 teaspoon salt
- 1/8 teaspoon pepper
- 2 cans (10 3/4 ounces each) cream of chicken soup, undiluted
- 12 ounces pasteurized prepared cheese product, cubed (we used Velveeta®)

Bring first 6 ingredients to a boil in a Dutch oven. Cover, reduce heat, and simmer 15 minutes. Stir in soup, and return to a simmer. Add cheese, stirring until melted.
Yield: 6 1/2 cups soup
Prep: 5 minutes, **Cook:** 25 minutes

Speedy Sides

Asparagus: Drizzle blue cheese dressing over steamed asparagus and plum tomato slices; sprinkle with chopped parsley.

Broccoli: Steam broccoli, then top it with lemon juice, flavored mustard, and melted margarine.

Carrots: Season cooked carrot slices with honey and tarragon.

Coleslaw: Mix preshredded cabbage, chopped Red Delicious apple, and poppy seed dressing.

Mashed Potatoes: Stir minced garlic or chopped chives into cooked mashed potatoes.

Pineapple Slices: Broil or grill fresh pineapple slices brushed with a mixture of honey and cinnamon.

Spinach: Stir oregano and feta cheese into cooked chopped spinach.

Perfect for a morning meal on the run — or a late-night supper — this flavorful Tomato-Basil Brunch Pizza takes less than half an hour to prepare, from start to finish.

TOMATO-BASIL BRUNCH PIZZA

- 1 package (8 ounces) shredded pizza cheese, divided
- 1 Italian bread shell (16 ounces)
- 8 bacon slices, cooked and crumbled
- 4 plum tomatoes, thinly sliced
- 1/2 teaspoon freshly ground pepper
- 1 large egg
- 1/4 cup chopped fresh basil
- 2 tablespoons milk

Sprinkle half of cheese over bread shell; top with bacon, tomato, and pepper. Whisk together egg, basil, and milk; pour in center of pizza (it will spread to edges). Sprinkle with remaining cheese. Bake at 425 ° for 20 minutes or until egg mixture is set.

Yield: 4 to 6 servings
Prep: 8 minutes, **Bake:** 20 minutes

Banana Pudding Cake

Cake and pudding mixes lend a helping hand in the preparation of this dessert that's similar to pound cake.

- 1 package (18.25 ounces) yellow cake mix
- 1 package (3.4 ounces) vanilla instant pudding mix
- 4 large eggs
- 1 cup water
- 1/2 cup mashed ripe banana (about 1 medium)
- 1/4 cup vegetable oil

Combine all ingredients in a mixing bowl. Beat at medium speed with an electric mixer until blended. Pour into a greased 10-inch tube pan. Bake at 350° for 50 to 55 minutes or until a wooden pick inserted in center comes out clean. Cool in pan on a wire rack 15 minutes; remove from pan, and let cool completely on wire rack.
Yield: 1 (10-inch) cake
Prep: 10 minutes, **Bake:** 55 minutes

Chocolate Cherry Cake

Dessert can't be much easier than this double-chocolate cake made from staples and a couple of convenience products.

- 2 large eggs, lightly beaten
- 1 can (21 ounces) cherry pie filling
- 1 package (18.5 ounces) chocolate fudge cake
- 1 teaspoon almond extract
- 1 cup sugar
- 1/2 cup milk
- 1/3 cup butter or margarine
- 1 cup (6 ounces) semisweet chocolate morsels

Combine first 4 ingredients; pour into a lightly greased 13 x 9 x 2-inch pan. Bake at 375° for 30 to 35 minutes or until a wooden pick inserted in center comes out clean. Cool in pan on a wire rack. Combine sugar, milk, and butter in a saucepan; bring to a boil over medium heat, stirring often. Boil 3 minutes, stirring occasionally. Remove from heat. Add chocolate morsels, stirring until chocolate melts. Pour chocolate mixture over cake, spreading to edges of pan. Let stand until chocolate mixture is set.
Yield: 15 servings
Prep: 15 minutes, **Bake:** 38 minutes

Turkey Tetrazzini

- 3 bacon slices
- 1 small onion, chopped
- 1/2 green bell pepper, chopped
- 1/4 cup milk
- 1 can (10 3/4 ounces) cream of mushroom soup, undiluted
- 1 loaf (8 ounces) pasteurized prepared cheese product, cubed (we used Velveeta®)
- 2 cups chopped cooked turkey or chicken
- 8 ounces spaghetti, cooked
- 1 jar (2 ounces) diced pimiento, drained

Cook bacon in a skillet until crisp; drain, reserving 2 tablespoons drippings in pan. Crumble bacon, and set aside. Add onion and bell pepper to drippings; sauté 5 minutes or until tender. Stir in milk, soup, and cheese; cook, stirring constantly, until cheese melts. Stir in turkey, spaghetti, and pimiento. Spoon into a lightly greased 2-quart baking dish. Bake at 375° for 30 minutes or until thoroughly heated. Sprinkle with reserved bacon.
Yield: 4 servings
Prep: 25 minutes, **Bake:** 30 minutes

For an impressive hors d'oeuvre, arrange fresh fruit and crackers around a wheel of Warmed Cranberry Brie. (*Left*) Buy a prepackaged salad to accompany hearty Turkey Tetrazzini.

WARMED CRANBERRY BRIE

    2   rounds (10 ounces each) Brie cheese
    1   can (16 ounces) whole-berry cranberry sauce
 ¹/₄   cup firmly packed brown sugar
    2   tablespoons spiced rum (see Note)
 ¹/₂   teaspoon ground nutmeg
 ¹/₄   cup chopped pecans, toasted
        Assorted crackers
        Apple and pear slices

   Trim rind from top of each Brie, leaving a ¹/₄-inch border on top. Place Brie rounds on a baking sheet. Stir together cranberry sauce and next 3 ingredients; spread mixture evenly over top of Brie rounds. Sprinkle evenly with pecans. Bake Brie at 500° for 5 minutes. Serve with assorted crackers and apple and pear slices.
Yield: 2 rounds, 8 appetizer servings each
Prep: 10 minutes, **Bake:** 5 minutes
Note: 2 tablespoons orange juice may be substituted for spiced rum.

HAM-AND-POTATO CASSEROLE

    1   package (26 ounces) frozen shredded potatoes
    1   ham slice (1 pound), cut into bite-size pieces
    1   can (10³/₄ ounces) cream of potato soup, undiluted
 ¹/₂   teaspoon pepper
 ¹/₄   cup grated Parmesan cheese
    1   cup (4 ounces) shredded Cheddar cheese
        Paprika

   Combine first 4 ingredients in a large bowl; spoon ham mixture into a lightly greased 13 x 9 x 2-inch baking dish. Bake at 400° for 25 minutes; sprinkle with cheeses and paprika, and bake 5 additional minutes or until thoroughly heated.
Yield: 4 to 5 servings
Prep: 5 minutes, **Bake:** 30 minutes

STARRY SNACK MIX

- 2 packages (8 ounces each) crispy cereal squares snack mix
- 1 package (16 ounces) raisins
- 1 jar (12 ounces) honey-roasted peanuts
- 1 package (9.5 ounces) fish-shaped Cheddar cheese crackers

Combine all ingredients. Store in an airtight container.

Yield: 15 cups
Prep: 5 minutes

WHITE CHOCOLATE CANDY

- 1 pound vanilla-flavored candy coating
- 3 cups pretzel sticks, broken into 1-inch pieces
- 1 cup Spanish peanuts

Place candy coating in a microwave-safe bowl. Microwave at HIGH power 1 to 2 minutes or until coating melts, stirring twice. Add pretzels and peanuts, stirring to coat. Drop mixture by tablespoonfuls onto wax paper; let stand until firm.

Yield: 40 candies
Prep: 5 minutes, **Cook:** 2 minutes

MICROWAVE PRALINES

Pralines are easy to make using this microwave recipe. If your oven is 1000 watts, use the lower time option.

- 2 cups sugar
- 2 cups pecans, chopped
- 1 can (5 ounces) evaporated milk
- 1/4 cup butter or margarine
- 1 tablespoon vanilla extract

Combine all ingredients in a 2-quart microwave-safe liquid measuring cup. Microwave at HIGH power 5 to 6 minutes, stirring well. Microwave 5 to 6 more minutes, stirring well. Working rapidly, drop by tablespoonfuls onto wax paper; let stand until firm.

Yield: about 2 1/2 dozen
Prep: 10 minutes, **Cook:** 12 minutes

Keep plenty of munchies on hand. Our favorites include sweet-and-salty Starry Snack Mix and White Chocolate Candy, as well as Crispy Praline Cookies. (*Opposite*) Warm up on a cold winter day with Quick Bean Soup and fresh-from-the oven Butter-Me-Nots.

GINGERED PEACH CRISP

24 gingersnaps, crushed
1/4 cup firmly packed brown sugar
1 teaspoon ground cinnamon
2 tablespoons butter or margarine, cut up
2 cans (15 ounces each) peach slices
   in light syrup, drained
   Vanilla ice cream or frozen yogurt

Combine first 3 ingredients. Cut in butter with a pastry blender until mixture is crumbly. Arrange peach slices in a lightly greased 8-inch square baking dish; sprinkle with gingersnap mixture. Bake at 375° for 20 minutes or until thoroughly heated. Serve warm over vanilla ice cream.
Yield: 4 servings
Prep: 10 minutes, **Bake:** 20 minutes

CRISPY PRALINE COOKIES

1 cup all-purpose flour
1 cup firmly packed dark brown sugar
1 large egg
1 cup chopped pecans
1/2 cup butter, softened
1 teaspoon vanilla extract

Stir together all ingredients in a large bowl, blending well. Drop cookie dough by tablespoonfuls onto ungreased baking sheets. Bake at 350° for 13 to 15 minutes. Cool on baking sheets 1 minute; remove cookies to wire racks to cool completely.
Yield: about 2 dozen cookies
Prep: 10 minutes, **Bake:** 15 minutes, **Cool:** 1 minute
Note: For Crispy Praline-Chocolate Chip Cookies, add 1 cup semisweet chocolate morsels to above ingredients; bake as directed.

BALSAMIC MARINATED OLIVES

This make-ahead recipe can be easily halved.

2 jars (8 ounces each) ripe olives, drained
2 jars (7 ounces each) kalamata olives, drained
2 jars (7 ounces each) pimiento-stuffed olives, drained
1/2 cup olive oil
1/2 cup balsamic vinegar
1 tablespoon Italian seasoning

Combine all ingredients; cover and chill at least 8 hours. Let stand 30 minutes at room temperature before serving. Serve with a slotted spoon.
Yield: 6 cups olives
Prep: 10 minutes, **Chill:** 8 hours, **Stand:** 30 minutes

QUICK BEAN SOUP

1 large onion, chopped
1 small green bell pepper, chopped
2 teaspoons vegetable oil
1 can (16 ounces) kidney beans, rinsed and drained
1 can (15 ounces) pinto beans, rinsed and drained
1 can (15 ounces) black beans, rinsed and drained
2 cans (14 1/2 ounces each) stewed tomatoes, undrained
1 can (14 1/2 ounces) chicken broth
1 cup picante sauce
1 teaspoon ground cumin

Sauté onion and bell pepper in hot oil in a large saucepan until tender. Add kidney beans and remaining ingredients; bring to a boil. Cover, reduce heat, and simmer 10 minutes.
Yield: 10 cups soup
Prep: 15 minutes, **Cook:** 15 minutes

BUTTER-ME-NOTS

Just stir the three ingredients and bake. Muffins don't get any better than this!

2 cups self-rising flour
1 carton (8 ounces) sour cream
1 cup butter, melted

Combine all ingredients. Spoon batter into lightly greased miniature (1 3/4-inch) muffin pans, filling full. Bake at 400° for 15 minutes or until golden.
Yield: 3 dozen
Prep: 5 minutes, **Bake:** 15 minutes

appetizing buffet

For an evening of good cheer and great food, invite friends and neighbors to drop in for an informal open house. A casual menu of make-ahead appetizers and finger foods leaves you plenty of time to join the festivities!

Merry morsels: Dinner roll-size **Pork Tenderloin Sandwiches with Bourbon Sauce** are hearty enough for larger appetites. Set out a variety of zesty **Marinated Vegetables** for nibbling.

Pork Tenderloin Sandwiches with Bourbon Sauce

Help a friend prepare for a party: you marinate the pork tenderloins, make and bottle the Bourbon Sauce, and then let the host do the rest.

    2   pork tenderloins (3/4 pound each)
    3   garlic cloves, slivered
  1/3   cup peanut oil
  1/4   cup bourbon
    1   tablespoon Worcestershire sauce
    1   tablespoon dried rosemary
    1   teaspoon Greek seasoning
        Bourbon Sauce
    3   dozen yeast rolls, split

Cut several small slits in pork; stuff garlic into slits. Combine oil and next 4 ingredients in a shallow dish; add pork. Cover and chill 2 hours, turning occasionally.

Bake at 325° for 55 minutes or until a meat thermometer inserted into thickest portion registers 160°. Remove from oven; cool. Cut into 1/4-inch-thick slices. Pour Bourbon Sauce over pork; cover and chill thoroughly. Serve pork on split rolls.

Yield: 3 dozen appetizers

Entertaining Ideas

1. Light the path to your door with glowing lanterns or luminarias. If you'd like to make your own hanging lanterns, see page 60 for a nifty idea!

2. Play plenty of Christmas tunes, but don't let the music "drown out" the conversation. If you've got a multiple-disc CD player, put in your favorites and set it on random play.

3. Serve food and beverages buffet-style and let guests help themselves. Make sure you've got plenty of plates, cutlery, napkins, cups, and ice close at hand!

Bourbon Sauce

    1   cup ketchup
  1/2   cup firmly packed dark brown sugar
  1/2   cup bourbon
    2   tablespoons Worcestershire sauce
  1 1/2 teaspoons Greek seasoning
    1   teaspoon garlic salt

Stir together ketchup and next 5 ingredients.

Yield: 2 cups sauce

Marinated Vegetables

    1   cup red wine vinegar
  1/2   cup vegetable oil
  1/2   cup olive oil
    1   tablespoon salt
    1   teaspoon garlic powder
    1   teaspoon cracked pepper
    1   teaspoon dried oregano
    1   package (10 ounces) frozen brussels sprouts
    2   green bell peppers
    1   yellow onion
    2   zucchini
    4   small yellow squash
    1   pound fresh broccoli
    1   can (5.75 ounces) jumbo pitted ripe olives, drained
    1   jar (7 ounces) jumbo pimiento-stuffed olives, drained
    1   can (14 ounces) quartered artichoke hearts, drained
    1   package (8 ounces) fresh small mushrooms
    1   pint cherry tomatoes

Combine first 7 ingredients in a saucepan; bring to a boil. Remove from heat; cool. Cook brussels sprouts according to package directions; drain. Cut bell peppers into thin strips. Slice onion, zucchini, and yellow squash; separate onion into rings. Cut broccoli into flowerets. Place vinegar mixture and vegetables in a large zip-top plastic bag. Seal and chill 8 hours, turning mixture occasionally.

Add mushrooms and tomatoes, and toss gently. Serve vegetables immediately.

Yield: 20 to 25 appetizer servings

To cut down on traffic jams at the buffet, set up "snack stations" in different areas. Guests will love dunking gingersnaps and fruit slices (brush fruit with lemon juice to prevent discoloration) into creamy Pumpkin Pie Dip. For a milder flavor, adjust the seasonings when making fiery Hot Peanuts.

PUMPKIN PIE DIP

    1 package (8 ounces) cream cheese,
         softened
    2 cups powdered sugar
    1 can (15 ounces) pumpkin pie filling
    1 teaspoon ground cinnamon
  ¹/₂ teaspoon ground ginger
         Gingersnaps
         Apples and pears, cored and sliced

Beat cream cheese and sugar at medium speed with an electric mixer until smooth. Add pie filling, cinnamon, and ginger, beating well. Cover and chill 8 hours. Serve with gingersnaps and apple and pear slices.
Yield: 3 cups dip

HOT PEANUTS

    1 tablespoon dried crushed red pepper
    3 tablespoons olive oil
    4 garlic cloves, pressed
    1 can (12 ounces) cocktail peanuts
    1 can (12 ounces) Spanish peanuts
    1 teaspoon salt
  ¹/₂ teaspoon chili powder

Cook crushed red pepper in hot oil in a large skillet 1 minute. Stir in garlic and peanuts; cook over medium heat, stirring constantly, 5 minutes. Remove from heat; sprinkle with salt and chili powder. Drain on paper towels; cool completely. Store in an airtight container.
Yield: 4 cups peanuts

Make Nutty Fruit-and-Cheese Spread even more festive — try shaping it in a holiday mold such as a tree, a bell, or a wreath. Garnish with whole dried apricots and serve with crackers or Melba toast rounds.

NUTTY FRUIT-AND-CHEESE SPREAD

Make spread up to two days before the event.

- 1 cup boiling water
- ¼ cup chopped dried apricots
- 4 cups (16 ounces) shredded Monterey Jack cheese
- 1 package (8 ounces) cream cheese, softened
- ½ teaspoon seasoned salt
- ⅓ cup milk
- ⅓ cup golden raisins
- ¼ cup chopped dates
- ¾ cup chopped walnuts, toasted
  Crackers

Pour 1 cup boiling water over apricots; let stand 30 minutes. Drain well. Combine cheeses, salt, and milk in a bowl; beat at medium speed with an electric mixer until smooth. Stir in apricots, raisins, dates, and walnuts. Line a 1-quart mold with plastic wrap. Spoon cheese mixture into mold, pressing firmly; cover and chill at least 3 hours.

Unmold onto serving dish, and remove plastic wrap. Let stand at room temperature 30 minutes before serving. Serve with crackers.

Yield: 4 cups spread

CRABMEAT BITES

- 1 pound fresh backfin crabmeat, drained and flaked
- 1/4 cup mayonnaise
- 1 large egg
- 2 tablespoons lemon juice
- 2 tablespoons finely chopped onion
- 2 tablespoons finely chopped red bell pepper
- 2 tablespoons finely chopped celery
- 1/2 teaspoon paprika
- 1/2 teaspoon dry mustard
- 1/2 teaspoon minced garlic
- 1/4 teaspoon salt
- 1/4 to 1/3 cup fine, dry breadcrumbs
- 2/3 cup commercial cracker meal
  Vegetable oil

Combine crabmeat and next 10 ingredients in a large bowl, stirring well. Stir in dry breadcrumbs until crabmeat mixture holds shape when formed into a ball. Shape crabmeat mixture into balls, using about 1 tablespoon of mixture per ball, and coat each ball evenly with cracker meal. Pour oil to depth of 3 inches into a Dutch oven; heat to 375°. Fry crabmeat balls, a few at a time, 2 minutes or until golden. Drain on paper towels.
Yield: 3 dozen appetizers

CHRISTMAS SPRITZERS

- 2 cans (12 ounces each) frozen cranberry juice concentrate, thawed and undiluted
- 2 bottles (750 milliliters each) White Zinfandel, chilled (see Note)
- 1/4 cup Angostura bitters
- 1 bottle (10 ounces) club soda, chilled
  Garnishes: maraschino cherries and orange curls

Combine first 3 ingredients in a pitcher; cover and chill. Add club soda just before serving. Serve over ice. Garnish, if desired.
Yield: 10 1/2 cups beverage
Note: Substitute 2 bottles (23 ounces each) chilled sparkling mineral water for wine, if desired.

Crispy **Crabmeat Bites** are tiny versions of an Eastern Seaboard staple. Prepare the mixture ahead of time, then coat and deep-fry just before serving. Add a little sparkle to the evening with fruity **Christmas Spritzers**.

CARAMEL POUND CAKE

   1   cup butter or margarine, softened
   1   cup firmly packed dark brown sugar
   1   cup firmly packed light brown sugar
   1   cup sugar
   1/2 cup vegetable oil
   5   large eggs
   3   cups all-purpose flour
   1/2 teaspoon baking powder
   1/2 teaspoon salt
   1   cup milk
   1/2 teaspoon vanilla extract
       Caramel Frosting

Beat butter at medium speed with an electric mixer until creamy; gradually add sugar, beating until blended. Add oil, and beat until blended. Add eggs, 1 at a time, beating just until yellow disappears. Combine flour, baking powder, and salt; add to butter mixture alternately with milk, beginning and ending with flour mixture. Beat at low speed just until blended after each addition. Stir in vanilla extract. Pour batter into a greased and floured 10-inch tube pan. Bake at 325° for 1 hour and 15 minutes or until a wooden pick inserted in center comes out clean. Cool in pan on wire rack 10 minutes; remove from pan, and cool on wire rack. Drizzle with Caramel Frosting.
Yield: 1 (10-inch) cake

CARAMEL FROSTING

   1   package (16 ounces) light brown sugar
   1/2 cup butter or margarine
   1   can (5 ounces) evaporated milk
   1/8 teaspoon salt
   1/2 teaspoon baking powder
   1/2 teaspoon vanilla extract

Bring first 4 ingredients to a boil in a medium saucepan, stirring often. Boil, stirring constantly, 3 minutes. Remove from heat; add baking powder and vanilla. Beat at medium speed with an electric mixer 5 to 9 minutes or until thickened. Drizzle quickly over cake.
Yield: 2 cups frosting

Don't forget the dessert table! No one can resist moist **Caramel Pound Cake** generously topped with **Caramel Frosting**. Rich, creamy **Coffee-Eggnog Punch** is spiked with coffee liqueur for added flavor.

AMARETTO-WALNUT BROWNIES

   1   cup coarsely chopped walnuts, toasted
   1/2 cup almond liqueur
   1   cup butter
   8   squares (1 ounce each) unsweetened chocolate
   5   large eggs
   3 1/3 cups sugar
   1/4 cup Swiss mocha instant coffee mix
   1   tablespoon vanilla extract
   1 2/3 cups all-purpose flour
   1/8 teaspoon salt
       Garnish: toasted walnut halves

Soak chopped walnuts in liqueur 4 to 6 hours. Drain, discarding liqueur. Melt butter and chocolate in a heavy saucepan over low heat. Beat eggs, sugar, and Swiss mocha at medium-high speed with an electric mixer 8 minutes. Gradually add chocolate mixture, beating at low speed until blended. Gradually add vanilla, flour, and salt, beating until blended. Stir in chopped walnuts. Pour into a lightly greased aluminum foil-lined 13 x 9-inch pan. Bake at 350° for 30 to 35 minutes. Cool on a wire rack. Cut into squares. Garnish, if desired.
Yield: 15 to 18 brownies

COFFEE-EGGNOG PUNCH

Stir in coffee with commercial eggnog for a smooth holiday punch.

   2   cartons (1 quart each) commercial
       refrigerated eggnog
   1/4 cup firmly packed brown sugar
   2   tablespoons instant coffee granules
   1/4 teaspoon ground cinnamon
   1   cup brandy
   1/4 cup Kahlúa or other coffee-flavored liqueur
   1   cup whipping cream
   1/4 cup sifted powdered sugar
   1   teaspoon vanilla extract
       Whipped cream
       Ground cinnamon

Combine first 4 ingredients in a large bowl; beat at low speed with an electric mixer until coffee granules dissolve. Stir in brandy and Kahlúa; chill 1 to 2 hours.

Pour into a punch bowl. Combine whipping cream, powdered sugar, and vanilla; beat at high speed until stiff peaks form. Dollop whipped cream onto punch; sprinkle lightly with additional cinnamon.
Yield: 9 1/2 cups punch

Romancing CHRISTMAS

A sprinkling of stars in the sky, a flickering fire, an intimate table for two … what a wonderful setting for romance! Set aside an evening during the holidays to share a candlelight dinner with that special someone.

For an elegant yet satisfying meal that's sizzling with flavor, may we recommend spicy Fillet of Beef with Red Pepper Butter, accompanied by **Three-Cheese Mashed Potatoes** and chilled Sesame Asparagus.

GINGER-MARINATED SHRIMP AND SCALLOPS

    6 unpeeled large fresh shrimp
    3 cups water
    2 ounces bay scallops
2 1/2 tablespoons rice wine vinegar
    1 tablespoon finely chopped green onions
1 1/2 teaspoons soy sauce
  1/2 teaspoon dark sesame oil
  1/4 teaspoon garlic powder
  1/8 teaspoon ground ginger
    1 cup shredded fresh spinach

Peel and devein shrimp, leaving tails intact. Bring water to a boil in a small saucepan. Add shrimp and scallops; cook 2 minutes or until shrimp turns pink. Drain well, and set aside. Combine vinegar and next 5 ingredients in a small heavy-duty, zip-top plastic bag; add shrimp and scallops. Seal bag, and shake until seafood is well coated. Marinate in refrigerator 1 hour, turning bag occasionally.

Remove seafood from marinade, reserving marinade. Place 1/2 cup spinach on each serving plate. Arrange shrimp and scallops evenly on spinach; drizzle with marinade.
Yield: 2 appetizers

SUN-DRIED TOMATO BRUSCHETTA

    4 slices (1 ounce each) French bread (1/2 inch thick)
  1/4 cup sun-dried tomatoes
    1 teaspoon olive oil
    1 tablespoon minced onion
    1 tablespoon minced green pepper
    2 tablespoons water
    1 tablespoon dry white wine
  1/4 teaspoon garlic powder
  1/4 teaspoon dried basil
  1/8 teaspoon ground red pepper
    2 teaspoons freshly grated Parmesan cheese, divided

Place bread slices on an ungreased baking sheet. Bake at 450° for 5 minutes or until lightly browned. Place tomatoes in a small saucepan; cover with water. Bring to a boil; cook, uncovered, 2 minutes. Drain well. Cut tomatoes into very thin slices; set aside. Add oil to pan; place over medium-high heat until hot. Add onion and green pepper; sauté until tender. Stir in tomatoes, water, and next 4 ingredients. Bring to a boil; reduce heat, and simmer, uncovered, 5 minutes or until liquid is absorbed. Spread tomato mixture evenly over toasted bread slices. Sprinkle 1/2 teaspoon cheese on each slice.
Yield: 4 appetizers

FILLET OF BEEF WITH RED PEPPER BUTTER

  1/3 cup butter, softened
  1/4 cup finely chopped red bell pepper
  1/4 to 1/2 teaspoon ground red pepper
  3/4 teaspoon seasoned salt
    2 beef tenderloin fillets (2 1/2 inches thick)

Combine first 4 ingredients, stirring well. Shape into 4 (2-inch) rounds on a wax paper-lined baking sheet; cover and refrigerate 1 hour or until firm.

Place beef tenderloin fillets on a rack in a broiler pan. Broil 6 inches from heat (with electric oven door partially open) 6 minutes. Turn fillets over, and top each with a butter round. Broil 6 to 7 minutes or until a meat thermometer registers 145° (rare), 160° (medium), or to desired degree of doneness. Turn fillets over, and transfer to a serving platter; top with remaining butter rounds.
Yield: 2 servings

THREE-CHEESE MASHED POTATOES

Prepare mashed potatoes ahead of time and chill, then bake in time to serve for dinner.

    2 large potatoes, peeled and cubed (see Note)
  1/2 cup sour cream
    1 package (3 ounces) cream cheese, softened
    2 tablespoons butter or margarine, softened
  1/3 cup milk
  1/4 cup (1 ounce) shredded sharp Cheddar cheese
  1/4 cup (1 ounce) shredded Muenster cheese
    1 teaspoon salt
  1/2 teaspoon pepper
    1 tablespoon butter or margarine, cut up
       Garnish: minced fresh chives

Cook potatoes in boiling water to cover 15 minutes or until tender; drain. Beat potatoes, sour cream, cream cheese, and 2 tablespoons butter at medium speed with an electric mixer until smooth. Stir in milk and next 4 ingredients. Spoon into a lightly greased 1 1/2-quart baking dish; dot with 1 tablespoon butter. Cover and chill, if desired; remove from refrigerator, and let stand 30 minutes.

Bake at 400° for 15 to 20 minutes or until thoroughly heated. Garnish, if desired.
Yield: 2 servings
Note: Frozen mashed potatoes may be substituted. Prepare potatoes according to package directions for 4 servings. Use leftover potatoes for breaded and fried potato pancakes.

Creamy, melt-in-your-mouth Chocolate-Amaretto Pudding provides an irresistible temptation to indulge in dessert.

SESAME ASPARAGUS

$^1/_2$ pound fresh asparagus
 3 tablespoons red wine vinegar
 1 tablespoon dark sesame oil
 1 tablespoon sesame seeds, toasted

Snap off tough ends of asparagus; remove scales with a vegetable peeler, if desired. Cover and cook asparagus in a small amount of boiling water 2 minutes or until crisp-tender. Drain and rinse with cold water; drain well. Combine vinegar, oil, and sesame seeds in a large heavy-duty, zip-top plastic bag; add asparagus. Seal and chill 2 hours, turning occasionally.

Remove asparagus from marinade, reserving marinade. Arrange asparagus on plates; drizzle with marinade.
Yield: 2 servings

CHOCOLATE-AMARETTO PUDDING

If you prefer not to use amaretto, simply omit it from the recipe. You'll still get a smooth, rich-tasting chocolate pudding.

$4^1/_2$ tablespoons sugar
 2 tablespoons unsweetened cocoa
 2 tablespoons cornstarch
$^1/_8$ teaspoon salt
$1^1/_2$ cups 1% low-fat milk
$1^1/_2$ teaspoons amaretto
$^1/_2$ teaspoon vanilla extract
 1 tablespoon slivered almonds, toasted

Combine first 4 ingredients in a small saucepan. Gradually add milk, stirring with a wire whisk until smooth. Cook over medium-low heat, stirring constantly, 8 to 10 minutes or until mixture is thickened. Remove from heat; stir in amaretto and vanilla. Spoon mixture evenly into 2 dessert dishes; cover and chill thoroughly. Just before serving, sprinkle evenly with almonds.
Yield: 2 servings

the Melting Pot

America has long been known
as the "melting pot" of the world,
blending the people and customs of
many different countries into a culture
all its own. Try incorporating a few
of these international recipes into
your family's Yuletide traditions!

Colorful French Fried Oyster
and Pear Salad teams crisp fruit
slices with tender shellfish and
a lightly sweetened vinaigrette, and
a flavorful filling adds to the appeal
of this Czechoslovakian Cheddar-
Apple Vanocka. In Germany, fruited
wine punch, or Bole, is traditionally
served for special occasions.

CHEDDAR-APPLE VANOCKA

This version of vanocka, a traditional braided Czechchoslovakian Christmas bread, is laced with golden saffron threads, but it's the apple and cheese filling that'll make you cut that second slice.

8 to 9 cups all-purpose flour, divided
3/4 cup sugar
2 teaspoons salt
1 envelope (1/4 ounce) active dry yeast
2 1/2 cups water
1/4 teaspoon saffron threads, crumbled
1/2 cup shortening
1 large egg
Cheddar-Apple Filling
1 large egg, lightly beaten
1/2 cup apple jelly, melted
1/4 cup powdered sugar

Combine 3 cups all-purpose flour, sugar, salt, and yeast in a large mixing bowl; stir well. Combine water, saffron, and shortening; heat in a saucepan until mixture reaches 120° (shortening does not need to melt completely). Add liquid mixture to flour mixture, beating well at medium speed with a heavy-duty mixer using the paddle attachment. Add 1 egg and 1 cup flour. Beat at low speed 1 minute; then beat at medium-high speed for 3 minutes. Stir in enough remaining flour to make a soft dough. Turn dough out onto a lightly floured surface, and knead until smooth and elastic (about 10 minutes). Shape dough into a ball; place in a well-greased bowl, turning to grease top. Cover and let rise in a warm place (85°), free from drafts, 45 minutes or until doubled in bulk.

Punch dough down, and divide in half. Set half of dough aside (cover to prevent drying). Divide remaining half of dough into 4 equal portions. Combine 3 portions; knead 2 or 3 times on a lightly floured surface. Cover and set aside remaining portion of dough. Roll larger portion into a 13 x 10-inch rectangle; transfer to a lightly greased baking sheet. Spoon half of Cheddar-Apple Filling in a 4-inch-wide strip across center of dough, leaving 3 inches on each side. With a sharp knife, slit dough at 1-inch intervals along each side of filling. Fold strips over filling, alternating from side to side, tucking ends in. Divide reserved smaller portion of dough into thirds. Shape each third into a 14-inch rope; pinch ends together at one end to seal. Braid ropes; pinch loose ends to seal. Brush top of apple-filled braid lightly with 1 beaten egg; place smaller braid across top of larger braid. Brush smaller braid with egg. Tuck ends of smaller braid under bottom edge of larger braid, pinching to seal. (Place a wooden pick though braids at both ends to prevent separation during rising and baking.) Repeat rolling, cutting, filling, and braiding procedures with remaining half of dough and filling. Cover and let loaves rise in a warm place, free from drafts, for 5 to 10 minutes (short rising time keeps loaf a pretty shape).

Bake at 350° for 25 to 30 minutes or until lightly browned. Transfer to a wire rack; remove wooden picks, and cool. Brush with melted apple jelly; cool. Sift powdered sugar over loaves before serving.
Yield: 2 loaves bread

CHEDDAR-APPLE FILLING

1/4 cup butter or margarine
1 cup firmly packed light brown sugar
3 1/2 cups peeled, chopped Granny Smith apple (about 3 apples)
2 tablespoons cornstarch
2 tablespoons water
1 1/2 cups (6 ounces) shredded sharp Cheddar cheese

Melt butter in a large saucepan over medium-low heat, stirring often. Stir in brown sugar until blended. Add chopped apple; bring to a boil, stirring constantly. Reduce heat to medium-low, and simmer, uncovered, 20 minutes or until apple is soft. Stir together cornstarch and water. Stir cornstarch mixture into apple filling; cook 1 minute or until mixture thickens. Remove from heat. Cool completely. Stir in cheese.
Yield: about 2 cups filling

FRIED OYSTER AND PEAR SALAD

This showy French salad has much to offer — fresh greens, juicy pears, crisp fried oysters, and a honey-balsamic vinaigrette. It's also good without oysters.

3/4 cup olive oil
1/3 cup white balsamic vinegar
2 tablespoons honey
1 teaspoon herbes de Provence
1/2 teaspoon salt
1/4 teaspoon pepper
3/4 cup yellow cornmeal
1/4 cup all-purpose flour
3/4 teaspoon salt
2 containers (12 ounces each) fresh Select oysters, drained
Vegetable oil
8 cups loosely packed gourmet mixed salad greens
3 green onions, thinly sliced
3 ripe red Bartlett pears, unpeeled and thinly sliced

Whisk together first 6 ingredients; set aside. Combine cornmeal, flour, and 3/4 teaspoon salt. Dredge oysters in cornmeal mixture. Pour oil to depth of 2 inches into a Dutch oven; heat to 375°. Fry oysters, a few at a time, 2 minutes or until golden, turning once. Drain on paper towels. Set aside, and keep warm. Arrange greens, green onions, pear slices, and oysters on individual plates. Drizzle dressing over salads. Serve immediately.
Yield: 8 servings
Note: Fry the oysters ahead; then reheat them just before serving in a 450° oven for 3 to 5 minutes or until crisp.

Hailing from the sunny Mediterranean, this savory **Greek Lemon Lamb Rack** is basted with a minty glaze for added flavor. Ask your butcher for a French rack (this means that the bone tips are exposed), with the chine, or backbone, cracked for easier carving.

BOLE

This is a classic German wine punch that's perfect for holiday celebrations.

    1 bottle (750 milliliters) dry white wine
    1 can (20 ounces) pineapple chunks, drained
    3 tablespoons brandy
  $^1/_3$ cup sugar
    2 quarts dry champagne, chilled

Stir together first 4 ingredients in a large pitcher; cover and chill 8 hours. Add champagne just before serving.
Yield: about $3^1/_2$ quarts punch

GREEK LEMON LAMB RACK

    2 lamb rib roasts ($1^1/_2$ to $2^1/_2$ pounds each), trimmed
    2 garlic cloves, thinly sliced
  $^2/_3$ cup honey
  $^1/_2$ cup firmly packed brown sugar
  $^1/_2$ cup fresh lemon juice
  $^1/_2$ teaspoon garlic salt
    2 teaspoons grated lemon rind
    2 teaspoons dried mint flakes
  $^1/_2$ cup finely chopped walnuts

Make 1-inch-deep cuts in lamb; insert garlic slices. Place lamb roasts in a shallow roasting pan, fat side out and ribs crisscrossed. Bake at 400° for 20 minutes. Stir together honey and next 3 ingredients in a small saucepan; cook over low heat until bubbly, stirring until sugar dissolves. Remove from heat; stir in lemon rind, mint, and walnuts. Remove lamb from oven. Cool slightly. Cover exposed bones with strips of aluminum foil to prevent excessive browning. Spoon lemon glaze over lamb. Reduce oven to 375°; bake 20 to 25 more minutes or until a meat thermometer inserted into thickest portion registers 150° or to desired degree of doneness, basting occasionally with glaze. Serve lamb immediately.
Yield: 8 servings

CHOCOLATE LINZERTORTE

This elegant torte, which originated in Linz, Austria, boasts a raspberry jam filling encased in a buttery chocolate-almond lattice crust.

- ³/₄ cup butter, softened
- ¹/₂ cup sugar
- 3 egg yolks
- 2 cups all-purpose flour
- ¹/₄ teaspoon salt
- 1 teaspoon ground allspice
- 3 squares (1 ounce each) semisweet chocolate, melted and cooled
- 1 cup whole natural almonds, toasted and ground
  Vegetable cooking spray
- 1 cup seedless raspberry jam
- 1 package (6 ounces) semisweet chocolate morsels
- ¹/₂ cup whipping cream, whipped

Beat butter at medium speed with an electric mixer until soft and creamy; gradually add sugar, beating well. Add egg yolks, beating well. Combine flour, salt, and allspice; add to butter mixture alternately with melted chocolate, beginning and ending with flour mixture. Stir in almonds. Divide dough in half. Roll half of dough between 2 sheets of wax paper to an 11-inch circle. Freeze 15 minutes. Press remaining half of dough into an 11-inch tart pan coated with cooking spray. Bake at 375° for 5 minutes. Stir jam well and spread over crust. Sprinkle with chocolate morsels. Remove top sheet of wax paper from frozen circle of dough; cut into ¹/₂-inch-wide strips, using a fluted pastry wheel. Arrange strips in lattice design over torte, sealing ends of strips to prebaked crust. Bake at 375° for 20 to 25 minutes. Let cool completely in pan on a wire rack. Serve torte at room temperature with whipped cream.
Yield: 1 (11-inch) torte

OLIVE SALAD APPETIZER

Use premium Greek or Italian olives for the best flavor results. You can make the salad ahead and store it in the refrigerator, but wait until just before serving to stir in mushrooms. Serve trays of extra olives for your family to nibble on while working in the kitchen.

- 12 green olives, pitted and freshly chopped
- 12 kalamata olives, pitted and finely chopped
- 1 anchovy, finely chopped
- 3 tablespoons extra-virgin olive oil
- 1/4 cup diced purple onion
- 1/4 cup finely chopped fresh parsley
- 2 teaspoons finely grated lemon rind
- 1/4 teaspoon freshly ground pepper
- 1 jar (4 ounces) marinated mushrooms, drained and finely chopped
- 1 celery rib, finely chopped
- 1 garlic clove, minced
  Bagel chips

Stir together all ingredients (see Note). Serve at room temperature with bagel chips.
Yield: 1 1/4 cups
Note: You can chop the ingredients for this salad in a food processor or mini chopper to save time; however, we prefer the texture and appearance achieved from chopping the ingredients by hand in this recipe.

Elegant yet simple to make, our **Chocolate Linzertorte** is a delightful variation of a favorite Austrian pastry. *(Right)* Children in the Netherlands know these buttery slice-and-bake cookies as **Speculaasjes Koekjes**, or "Santa Claus Cookies." Savory **Olive Salad Appetizer** is similar to a European tapenade.

SPECULAASJES KOEKJES (SANTA CLAUS COOKIES)

Surprise Santa with milk and these cookies — crispy with almonds and spicy with cinnamon, nutmeg, and cloves. Then you'll be sure to get everything on your list.

- 4 cups all-purpose flour
- 1/2 teaspoon baking soda
- 1/4 teaspoon salt
- 1 tablespoon plus 1 teaspoon ground cinnamon
- 1/2 teaspoon ground nutmeg
- 1/2 teaspoon ground cloves
- 2 cups butter or margarine, softened
- 2 cups sugar
- 1/2 cup sour cream
- 1/2 cup blanched slivered almonds, toasted and chopped

Combine first 6 ingredients in a large bowl; set aside. Beat butter at medium speed with an electric mixer until creamy; gradually add sugar, beating well. Add flour mixture to butter mixture alternately with sour cream, beginning and ending with flour mixture. Stir in almonds. Cover and chill 2 hours.

Divide dough in half; shape each portion into a 16-inch log. Wrap each log in wax paper. Chill at least 8 hours.

Unwrap logs; cut into 1/4-inch-thick slices. Place slices 2 inches apart on ungreased baking sheets. Bake at 375° for 6 to 8 minutes or until golden. Cool 1 minute on baking sheets; remove to wire racks, and let cool completely.
Yield: 8 dozen cookies

A Taste OF Elegance

The Christmas season is the perfect time to show hospitality — and share your culinary skills — by hosting an elegant dinner party. Our upscale menu offers everything you need, from a first course of oyster bisque to a dessert of chocolate roulage!

Set the table with your finest silver, light the candles, and offer a fabulous feast featuring savory stuffed pork chops accompanied by crispy roasted vegetables, creamy risotto, and fluffy yeast rolls.

OYSTER BISQUE

- ¹/₄ cup butter or margarine
- 3 garlic cloves, minced
- 2 shallots, finely chopped
- 3 tablespoons all-purpose flour
- 1 bottle (8 ounces) clam juice
- ¹/₂ cup dry sherry
- ¹/₄ cup lemon juice
- 1 tablespoon Worcestershire sauce
- ¹/₈ teaspoon hot sauce
- ¹/₄ teaspoon freshly ground pepper
- 1 quart whipping cream
- 2 containers (12 ounces each) fresh oysters, drained
  Freshly ground pepper (optional)

Melt butter in a large Dutch oven over medium heat; add garlic and shallots, and cook until tender, stirring often. Add flour, and cook 1 minute. Add clam juice, sherry, and lemon juice; cook 2 to 3 minutes or until thickened and bubbly. Stir in Worcestershire sauce and next 3 ingredients; add oysters, and cook over medium heat 10 minutes or until oysters are done, stirring occasionally.

Sprinkle servings with additional pepper, if desired.
Yield: 9 cups bisque

BEST HOT ROLLS

- ¹/₂ cup sugar
- ¹/₂ cup shortening
- 1³/₄ cups cold water
- 2 teaspoons salt
- 1 envelope (¹/₄ ounce) active dry yeast
- ¹/₄ cup warm water (100° to 110°)
- 1 large egg
- 5 to 5¹/₂ cups all-purpose flour

Cook first 4 ingredients in a medium saucepan over medium heat, stirring constantly, until shortening melts. Cool to 110°. Stir together yeast and ¹/₄ cup warm water in a 2-cup glass measuring cup; let stand 5 minutes. Beat yeast mixture, sugar mixture, egg, and 4 cups flour in a large mixing bowl at medium speed with an electric mixer until blended. Gradually stir in enough remaining flour to make a soft dough. Turn dough out onto a lightly floured surface, and knead until smooth and elastic (about 5 minutes). Place in a well-greased bowl, turning to grease top. Cover and let rise in a warm place (85°), free from drafts, 1 hour or until doubled in bulk. Punch dough down; cover and chill 8 hours.

Pinch off small pieces of dough (with well-greased hands), and shape into 1-inch balls. Arrange in 2 greased 9-inch square pans. Cover and let rise in a warm place, free from drafts, 30 minutes or until doubled in bulk.

Bake at 400° for 20 minutes or until golden.
Yield: 50 rolls
Note: To make ahead, bake rolls at 400° for 12 to 15 minutes or until just browned. Cool. Freeze up to 3 months. To reheat, bake rolls at 400° for 5 to 7 minutes or until golden.

Serve rich **Oyster Bisque** (*above*) as a prelude to the festivities. Guests won't miss the turkey when they taste Apricot-Mushroom Stuffed Pork Chops (*right*). Round out the meal with Onion Risotto, Roasted Brussels Sprouts and Carrots, and our **Best Hot Rolls**.

APRICOT-MUSHROOM STUFFED PORK CHOPS

Ask your butcher to cut pockets in the pork chops — it's one less thing you'll have to worry about.

4   tablespoons butter or margarine, divided
$^1/_2$ package (8 ounces) sliced fresh mushrooms
$^1/_4$ cup chopped onion
$^1/_4$ cup chopped celery
$^3/_4$ cup soft breadcrumbs
$^1/_3$ cup dried apricot halves, chopped
$^1/_3$ cup chopped fresh parsley
$^1/_2$ teaspoon rubbed sage
8   center-cut boneless pork loin chops (1 inch thick), cut with pockets
2   teaspoons salt
1   teaspoon freshly ground pepper
1   cup dry white wine

Melt 2 tablespoons butter in a large skillet over medium-high heat. Add mushrooms, onion, and celery; cook, stirring constantly, 5 minutes or until tender. Stir in breadcrumbs and next 3 ingredients; remove from heat. Sprinkle both sides and pocket of each pork chop with salt and pepper. Spoon vegetable mixture evenly into pockets. Melt remaining 2 tablespoons butter in skillet; add chops, and cook until browned, turning once. Place chops in a lightly greased roasting pan or large shallow baking dish; add white wine. Cover and bake at 350° for 45 minutes or until done.
Yield: 8 servings

ONION RISOTTO

- 3 large sweet onions, chopped
- 2 garlic cloves, pressed
- 1 teaspoon salt
- 2 tablespoons olive oil
- 1 package (16 ounces) Arborio rice
- 8 cups chicken broth, warmed
- 1 cup dry white wine
- ¹/₂ cup shredded Parmesan cheese
- 2 tablespoons butter or margarine

Sauté first 3 ingredients in hot oil in a Dutch oven over medium-high heat until tender. Add rice; cook, stirring constantly, 2 minutes. Reduce heat to medium; add 1 cup broth. Cook, stirring often, until liquid is absorbed. Repeat procedure with remaining chicken broth, 1 cup at a time. (Cooking time for the rice mixture is about 30 minutes.) Add wine; cook, stirring gently, until liquid is absorbed. Stir in cheese and butter. Serve immediately.
Yield: 6 servings

ROASTED BRUSSELS SPROUTS AND CARROTS

The key to crispy-roasted results here is using a large pan so vegetables aren't crowded during roasting. Roast the vegetables several hours before the meal, then reheat just before serving.

- 2 pounds fresh brussels sprouts
- 8 medium carrots, scraped and cut into 2-inch pieces
- ¹/₄ cup olive oil
- 1 tablespoon sugar
- 1 tablespoon chopped fresh thyme
- ¹/₂ teaspoon salt
  Freshly ground pepper

Trim ends of brussels sprouts and cut in half lengthwise. Place brussels sprouts and carrots in a large roasting pan. Combine remaining ingredients; pour over vegetables, and toss well. Cover and bake at 425° for 20 minutes. Uncover and roast 25 minutes or until vegetables are tender and well browned, stirring twice.
Yield: 6 servings

Bûche de Noël

Created by Parisian chefs in the late nineteenth century, the *Bûche de Noël*, or Yule log cake, was inspired by the custom of keeping a large log burning in the hearth throughout the Christmas season.

CHOCOLATE-CRANBERRY ROULAGE

- 1 tub (12 ounces) cranberry-raspberry or cranberry-orange crushed fruit
- ³/₄ cup cranberry juice cocktail
- 2 tablespoons powdered sugar
- 1¹/₂ tablespoons cornstarch
- 4 to 5 tablespoons crème de cassis or other black currant-flavored liqueur, divided (see Note)
- 2 cups whipping cream
  Chocolate Cake Rolls (recipe opposite)
  Cocoa
  Garnishes: fresh cranberries

Combine first 4 ingredients in container of an electric blender or food processor; process until smooth, stopping several times to scrape down sides. Pour mixture into a small saucepan; bring to a boil over medium heat, stirring constantly. Boil 1 minute, stirring constantly. Stir in 2 tablespoons crème de cassis; cool cranberry mixture. Beat whipping cream at medium-high speed with an electric mixer until soft peaks form. Fold in ²/₃ cup cranberry mixture; cover and refrigerate the remaining cranberry mixture to use as a garnish. Unroll cake rolls; brush each lightly with remaining 2 to 3 tablespoons crème de cassis. Spread half of whipped cream mixture over each cake. Reroll cakes without towels; place, seam side down, on a baking sheet. Cover and freeze cakes at least 1 hour or up to 3 months. Dust cakes with cocoa, and cut into 1- to 2-inch slices. Spoon remaining cranberry mixture evenly onto dessert plates. Top each with a cake slice. Garnish, if desired.
Yield: 2 filled cake rolls (5 to 6 servings each)
Note: Cranberry juice cocktail may be substituted for crème de cassis.

PRALINE COFFEE

- 3 cups hot brewed coffee
- ³/₄ cup half-and-half
- ³/₄ cup firmly packed light brown sugar
- 2 tablespoons butter or margarine
- ³/₄ cup praline liqueur
  Sweetened whipped cream
  Cocoa

Cook first 4 ingredients in a large saucepan over medium heat, stirring constantly, until thoroughly heated (do not boil). Stir in liqueur; serve with sweetened whipped cream. Sprinkle with cocoa, if desired.
Yield: about 6 cups coffee

A grand finale: Our Chocolate-Cranberry Roulage, a fruited version of the traditional *Bûche de Nöel*, is dusted with cocoa and served with cranberry-raspberry sauce. *(Opposite)* Top liqueur-laced Praline Coffee with sweetened whipped cream and a dusting of cocoa.

CHOCOLATE CAKE ROLLS

 Vegetable cooking spray
4 large eggs
1/2 cup water
1 package (18.25 or 18.5 ounces) Swiss chocolate, devil's food, or fudge cake mix
2 to 4 tablespoons cocoa

Coat 2 (15 x 10-inch) jellyroll pans with cooking spray; line with wax paper, and coat with cooking spray. Set aside. Beat eggs 5 minutes in a large mixing bowl at medium-high speed with an electric mixer. Add water, beating at low speed to blend. Gradually add cake mix, beating at low speed until moistened. Beat at medium-high speed

2 minutes. Divide batter in half, and spread batter evenly into prepared pans. (Layers will be thin.) Bake each cake at 350° on the middle rack in separate ovens for 13 minutes or until cake springs back when lightly touched in the center. (If you don't have a double oven, set 1 pan aside.) Sift 1 to 2 tablespoons cocoa in a 15 x 10-inch rectangle on a cloth towel; repeat with second towel. When cakes are done, immediately loosen from sides of pans, and turn each out onto a prepared towel. Peel off wax paper. Starting at narrow end, roll up each cake and towel together; place cakes, seam side down, on wire racks. Cool cakes completely.
Yield: 2 cake rolls

happy ENDINGS

Luscious cheesecake, rich crème brûlée, heavenly chocolate truffles, fruited shortbread … from grand finales to light finishing touches, we can provide happy endings for all your holiday meals.

With its delightful blend of tart and sweet flavors, **Cranberry Swirl Cheesecake with Sugar Cookie Crust** is sure to become a Christmas favorite. For a lighter finish, spoon frothy **Champagne Sabayon** over fresh berries.

CRANBERRY SWIRL CHEESECAKE WITH SUGAR COOKIE CRUST

Our test kitchen staff discovered that Pepperidge Farm Bordeaux® cookies make a great crumb crust.

2¼ cups Bordeaux cookie crumbs
¼ cup butter or margarine, melted
1 can (16 ounces) whole-berry cranberry sauce
2 teaspoons ground cinnamon
¼ teaspoon ground cloves
3 packages (8 ounces each) cream cheese, softened
1 cup sugar
1 tablespoon cornstarch
4 large eggs
1 teaspoon vanilla extract
Garnishes: fresh cranberries and mint

Combine cookie crumbs and melted butter; stir well. Press crumb mixture onto bottom and 1 inch up sides of a lightly greased 9-inch springform pan. Bake at 350° for 10 minutes. Let crust cool completely on a wire rack.

Position knife blade in food processor bowl. Add cranberry sauce and spices; process until smooth. Set aside. Beat cream cheese at medium speed with an electric mixer until smooth. Add sugar and cornstarch; beat well. Add eggs, 1 at a time, beating just until blended after each addition. Stir in vanilla. Pour half of batter into cookie crust; spoon ½ cup cranberry mixture over batter. Swirl gently with a knife. Top with remaining batter. Spoon ½ cup cranberry mixture over cheesecake, and swirl gently with a knife. Bake at 350° for 15 minutes. Reduce oven temperature to 325°. Bake 1 hour.

Remove from oven, and immediately run a knife around sides of cheesecake to loosen it from pan. Turn oven off; return cheesecake to oven, and let cool in oven 1 hour. Remove from oven; let cool completely in pan on a wire rack. Chill, uncovered, until ready to serve. (Cheesecake will continue to firm up as it chills.)

Remove sides of pan. Garnish, if desired. Serve cheesecake with remaining cranberry mixture, if desired.
Yield: 1 (9-inch) cheesecake.

CHAMPAGNE SABAYON

8 egg yolks
⅔ cup sugar
1½ cups champagne
1 pint fresh blackberries, blueberries, and strawberries

Whisk together egg yolks and sugar in a heavy saucepan over low heat until blended. Whisk in champagne; cook, whisking constantly, 10 minutes or until mixture reaches 160° and is thickened. Chill, if desired. Spoon champagne mixture over fresh berries.
Yield: 2¾ cups sauce

ORANGE DATE-NUT CAKE

It's such a rich cake that you don't need but a small slice.

1 cup butter or margarine, softened
4 cups sugar, divided
4 large eggs
4 cups all-purpose flour
1 teaspoon baking soda
1½ cups buttermilk
1 package (8 ounces) chopped, sugared dates
1 cup chopped walnuts, toasted
4 teaspoons grated orange rind, divided
1 cup orange juice

Beat butter at medium speed with an electric mixer until fluffy. Gradually add 2 cups sugar, beating well. Add eggs, 1 at a time, beating until blended after each addition. Combine flour and baking soda; add to butter mixture alternately with buttermilk, beginning and ending with flour mixture. Beat at low speed until blended after each addition. Stir in dates, walnuts, and 2 teaspoons orange rind. Pour batter into a greased and floured 10-inch tube pan. Bake at 350° for 1 hour and 10 minutes or until a wooden pick inserted in center comes out clean. Bring orange juice, remaining sugar, and remaining rind to a boil in a saucepan; cook, stirring constantly, 1 minute. Run a knife around edge of cake gently; punch holes in cake with a wooden pick. Drizzle glaze over warm cake. Let cool in pan on a wire rack.
Yield: 1 (10-inch) cake

CHOCOLATE-ORANGE TRUFFLES

Crushed cookies and ground almonds turn these truffles into a cookie-like treat.

1 sweet chocolate bar (4 ounces)
20 cream-filled chocolate sandwich cookies, crushed (about 2 cups crumbs)
1 cup ground almonds, toasted
3 tablespoons whipping cream
2 tablespoons orange liqueur
1 tablespoon finely chopped orange rind
1 tablespoon fresh orange juice
Powdered sugar
Toasted ground almonds
Cocoa

Melt chocolate in a heavy saucepan over low heat, stirring until smooth. Remove from heat; stir in cookie crumbs and next 5 ingredients. Shape mixture into 1-inch balls, washing hands as necessary. Cover and chill 20 minutes.

Roll balls in powdered sugar, ground almonds, or cocoa. Store in an airtight container in refrigerator.
Yield: 4 dozen truffles

If you'd rather linger over coffee than serve a heavy dessert, be sure to offer a tray of tempting tidbits like **Chocolate-Orange Truffles** and Raspberry Shortbread. For variety, coat the truffles with cocoa, powdered sugar, or chopped nuts, and try filling the shortbread with apricot or blackberry preserves!

RASPBERRY SHORTBREAD

These colorful butter cookies can be served for dessert or enjoyed with coffee or tea when holiday guests drop in for a special visit.

- 1 cup butter, softened
- $^2/_3$ cup sugar
- $2^1/_4$ cups all-purpose flour
- 1 jar (10 ounces) seedless raspberry jam
- 1 cup powdered sugar
- $1^1/_2$ tablespoons water
- $^1/_2$ teaspoon almond extract

Beat butter and $^2/_3$ cup sugar at medium speed with an electric mixer until light and fluffy. Gradually add flour, beating at low speed until blended. Divide dough into 6 equal portions, and roll each dough portion into a 12-inch-long x 1-inch-wide strip. Place 3 dough strips on each of 2 lightly greased baking sheets. Make a $^1/_2$-inch-wide x $^1/_4$-inch-deep indentation down center of each strip, using the handle of a wooden spoon. Bake, in 2 batches, at 350° for 15 minutes. Remove from oven, and spoon jam into indentations. Bake 5 more minutes or until lightly browned. Whisk together powdered sugar, $1^1/_2$ tablespoons water, and almond extract; drizzle over warm shortbread. Cut each strip diagonally into 12 (1-inch-wide) slices. Cool in pans on wire racks. Store in an airtight container.
Yield: 6 dozen cookies

COCONUT-FUDGE CAKE

2 1/4 cups sugar, divided
1 cup vegetable oil
2 large eggs
3 cups all-purpose flour
3/4 cup cocoa
2 teaspoons baking soda
2 teaspoons baking powder
1 1/2 teaspoons salt
1 cup brewed coffee or water
1 cup buttermilk
1/2 cup chopped pecans
2 teaspoons vanilla extract, divided
1 package (8 ounces) cream cheese, softened
1 large egg
1/2 cup flaked coconut
1 cup (6 ounces) semisweet chocolate morsels
Chocolate Glaze

Beat 2 cups sugar, oil, and 2 eggs at high speed with an electric mixer 1 minute. Combine flour and next 4 ingredients; combine coffee and buttermilk. Add flour mixture and coffee mixture to oil mixture. Beat at medium speed 3 minutes. Stir in nuts and half of vanilla. Pour half of batter into a greased, floured 12-cup Bundt pan. Beat cream cheese at medium speed until fluffy; gradually add 1 egg and remaining 1/4 cup sugar. Beat just until blended. Stir in remaining vanilla, coconut, and morsels; spoon over batter in pan, leaving a 1/2-inch border around center and edge. Top with remaining batter. Bake at 350° for 1hour or until a wooden pick inserted in center comes out clean. Cool in pan on a wire rack 15 minutes. Remove from pan; cool completely on wire rack. Drizzle with warm glaze.
Yield: 1 (10-inch) cake

CHOCOLATE GLAZE

2 tablespoons butter or margarine
1 cup powdered sugar
3 tablespoons cocoa
1 to 3 tablespoons hot water
2 teaspoons vanilla extract

Melt butter in a saucepan over low heat; stir in sugar and remaining ingredients.
Yield: about 1/2 cup glaze

DIVINITY CANDY

Topped with toasted pecans and sugared cherries, these traditional candies provide something for everyone.

1 package (7.2 ounces) home-style fluffy white frosting mix
1/2 cup boiling water
1/3 cup light corn syrup
2 teaspoons vanilla extract
1 package (16 ounces) powdered sugar
1 1/2 cups chopped pecans, toasted
Toasted pecan halves
Sugared Maraschino Cherries

Place first 4 ingredients in a 4-quart mixing bowl. Beat at low speed with a heavy-duty electric mixer 1 minute or until mixture is blended. Beat mixture at high speed 3 to 5 minutes or until stiff peaks form. Gradually add powdered sugar, beating at low speed until blended. Stir in chopped nuts. Drop mixture by rounded tablespoonfuls onto wax paper. Garnish half of candies with toasted pecan halves. For remainder of candies, press tip of a lightly greased wooden spoon handle into center of each piece of candy, making an indentation. Let candies stand 8 hours; remove to wire racks, and let stand 8 more hours or until bottom of candy is firm. Store in airtight containers. Place 1 Sugared Maraschino Cherry in each indentation just before serving.
Yield: 5 dozen candies

SUGARED MARASCHINO CHERRIES

30 maraschino cherries with stems, rinsed and well drained
1 1/3 cups powdered sugar
1/3 cup water
1 tablespoon meringue powder
1/2 cup sugar

Place cherries on paper towels, and let stand until completely dry.
Beat powdered sugar, 1/3 cup water, and meringue powder at medium speed with an electric mixer 2 to 3 minutes or until smooth and creamy. Brush cherries with meringue mixture, using a small paintbrush; sprinkle with sugar, and place on a wire rack. Let stand 2 to 3 hours or until dry.
Yield: 2 1/2 dozen cherries

Featuring a tunnel of creamy coconut filling, this moist, mocha-flavored Coconut-Fudge Cake is too delicious to save for a special occasion — and it's so easy to make that you won't have to!

Rich, buttery macadamias and sweet, chewy coconut bring a taste of the tropics to Coconut-Macadamia Nut Pie. Everyone will ask for seconds, so you'd better bake two!

COCONUT-MACADAMIA NUT PIE

- 1 cup sugar
- 3 large eggs
- 1 cup light corn syrup
- 1/4 cup whipping cream
- 1 tablespoon butter or margarine, melted
- 1 teaspoon vanilla extract
- 3/4 cup coarsely chopped macadamia nuts
- 1 cup flaked coconut
- 1 unbaked (9-inch) deep-dish frozen pastry shell
  Garnishes: whipped cream, chopped
    macadamia nuts, toasted flaked coconut

Whisk together sugar and next 5 ingredients; stir in nuts and coconut. Pour into unbaked piecrust. Bake at 350° for 25 minutes. Reduce heat to 325°; bake an additional 45 minutes, shielding if necessary. Cool on a wire rack. Garnish, if desired.
Yield: 1 (9-inch) pie

CRANBERRY-PEAR CRISP

- 2/3 cup sugar
- 2 teaspoons ground cinnamon
- 1 1/2 teaspoons ground ginger
- 1 1/2 cups fresh orange juice
- 1 package (12 ounces) fresh cranberries
- 6 pears, thinly sliced
- 2 teaspoons grated orange rind
- 1 1/2 cups uncooked regular oats
- 2/3 cup all-purpose flour
- 2/3 cup firmly packed brown sugar
- 1/2 cup butter or margarine
  Ice cream or whipped cream

Combine first 7 ingredients in a large saucepan; bring to a boil. Reduce heat, and simmer, stirring occasionally, 10 minutes or until cranberries pop and mixture thickens. Spoon evenly into a lightly greased 13 x 9-inch baking dish. Combine oats, flour, and brown sugar in a small bowl; cut in butter with a pastry blender until crumbly. Sprinkle over fruit mixture. Bake at 375° for 20 to 25 minutes or until lightly browned. Serve warm with ice cream or whipped cream.
Yield: 8 servings

BLACK-AND-WHITE CRÈME BRÛLÉE

2½ cups whipping cream, divided
1 cup semisweet chocolate morsels
5 egg yolks
½ cup sugar
1 tablespoon vanilla extract
3 tablespoons light brown sugar

Heat ½ cup whipping cream and chocolate morsels in a saucepan over low heat, stirring until chocolate melts. Cool slightly. Pour mixture evenly into 6 (6-ounce) round individual baking dishes. Set aside.

Whisk together remaining 2 cups whipping cream, egg yolks, ½ cup sugar, and vanilla until sugar dissolves and mixture is smooth. Pour evenly into prepared baking dishes; place dishes in a 13 x 9-inch baking dish. Add hot water to large dish to a depth of ½ inch. Bake at 275° for 1 hour and 30 minutes or until almost set. Cool custards in water in pan on a wire rack. Remove custards from pan; cover and chill at least 8 hours.

Sprinkle ½ tablespoon brown sugar over each custard; place custards in baking pan. Broil 5½ inches from heat until sugar melts. Let stand 5 minutes to allow sugar to harden.
Yield: 6 servings

French for "burnt cream," the term *crème brûlée* sounds fancy, but it's really just a simple chilled custard that's sprinkled with brown sugar and broiled to form a crispy topping. A layer of chocolate adds festive flavor to our Black-and-White Crème Brûlée.

Project Instructions

Christmas decorating has never been easier! Our easy-to-follow instructions guide you, step-by-step, as you craft handmade projects that will fill your home with customized appeal. Refer to the General Instructions on page 180 for extra "how-to" tips and techniques.

Natural By Design

PUMPKIN TOPIARY
(shown on page 8)

You will need a serrated knife, 36"h floral topiary form with a 10" dia. plastic foam ball top and foam base, flowerpot to fit topiary base, hot glue gun, long straight sticks (the length of the topiary trunk), floral wire and wire cutters, greening pins, natural items gathered from outdoors (we used assorted evergreen sprigs and branches, green and wild purple wheat, and persimmon branches), fresh green sheet moss, mounting tape, and a ghost pumpkin (to fit on top of topiary).

1. Use knife to cut top half off of topiary ball, creating a flat surface. Glue topiary base in pot.

2. Arrange sticks around topiary trunk; wrap and twist wire around top and bottom of sticks to secure in place.

3. Securing items with greening pins and working from bottom, cover rounded part of foam with natural items. Cover flat part of foam and base with moss. Using mounting tape on bottom of pumpkin to secure, place ghost pumpkin on top of topiary.

BOUNTIFUL WREATH
(shown on page 9)

Create a lavish focal area at the top of a pre-lit artificial evergreen wreath by layering and attaching natural items to the wreath. Our beautiful bounty consists of assorted fresh greenery, ornamental pumpkins and gourds, pinecones, green wheat stalks, cattails, and gooseberry and red milo berry branches.

Attach satin-finish glass ball ornaments to the top, then use lengths of twine to hang several ornaments in the center of the wreath. Tuck additional sprigs of fresh greenery in the wreath to add fullness.

Tips

To keep greenery fresh during the holidays, lightly spritz plants daily with water. Replace any withering greenery with fresh sprigs as needed.

To help your arrangements and decorations last longer, avoid puncturing the skin of items like gourds and pumpkins. Puncturing the fruit makes it wither faster.

DOOR SWAG
(shown on page 13)

You will need assorted fresh evergreen branches; twine; utility scissors; cattails; persimmon, gooseberry, beauty berry, and red milo berry branches; craft wire and wire cutters; floral foam cage with hanger; hot glue gun; ornamental pumpkins and gourds; and Christmas ornaments.

1. Gather the ends of a few evergreen branches in your hand and use twine to tie them together near the top. Repeat, layering more greenery, cattails, and persimmon, milo berry, beauty berry, and gooseberry branches at various lengths and angles, until desired size and shape of swag is achieved.

2. Wire bundle to foam cage. Add pumpkins, gourds, and ornaments to top of swag and secure in place with glue or wire.

AGED CONTAINERS

(shown on pages 8 and 12)

You will need a container (we used metal pails and clay pots); rust-colored spray primer; paintbrush; light green, tan, and green acrylic paint; natural sponge piece; stiff-bristle paintbrush; and matte acrylic spray sealer.

Allow primer, paint, and sealer to dry after each application. Refer to Painting Techniques, page 180, before beginning project.

1. Apply primer to container. Lightly *Dry Brush* container light green, allowing some of the primer to show through.

2. Dampen sponge piece lightly. Dip sponge into tan, then green paint and randomly *Sponge Paint* entire container, allowing bottom layers of primer and paint to show through in places. While paint is still wet, pull stiff-bristle brush from top to bottom of container to blend paint.

3. Apply sealer to container.

5. Norfolk Island Pine

3. Blue Point Juniper

4. Dwarf Alberta Spruce

2. Red Kalanchoe

1. White Cyclamen

8. Maidenhair Fern

10. Red Cyclamen

6. Green Dried Moss

7. Natural Dried Moss

9. Fresh Green Sheet Moss

Creating a tabletop garden is a nice way to bring the outdoors in for the holidays. Choose plants in various shades of green and red, and add accent colors to complement your décor. In our arrangement, shown on pages 10 and 11, the addition of natural dried moss, candles, and white cyclamen draws your attention to the variety of greens — keeping them from blending in with each other. The differing textures are also pleasing to the eye.

We recommend using candles with candleholders to keep the flames safe; adding hurricane globes also allows the candlelight to flicker and reflect in its glass cage, mimicking the lights on the trees.

When the season is over, return your plants to pots or add them to your garden to keep the memories of the holidays with you all year. Consult with your local nursery for the best times to plant outdoors.

Coffee plant

Gooseberries

Green Wheat and
Wild Purple Wheat

Beauty Berries

Cattail

Persimmons

Frazier Fir

Leyland Cypress

Common Cedar

Loblolly Pine

Dwarf Alberta Spruce

Colorado Blue Spruce

Pictured above are many of the plants that were used in creating this section. When you take a walk through the woods or your backyard to gather natural elements for decorating, select interesting and eye-catching objects.

Additional plants we used include: Norfolk Island Pine, Maidenhair Fern, Blue Point Juniper, Emerald Green Arborvitae, and Paperwhites.

Fresh Green
Sheet Moss

Cinderella and
Lumina Pumpkins

Norway Spruce

Red Cedar

Twigs

Red Kalanchoe

Natural and Green
Dried Moss

Pinecones and
Spanish Moss

White Cyclamen

Red Milo

Ornamental Gourds

Sugar Pumpkin

If you are unable to obtain the items we've suggested, consult your local Cooperative Extension Service or a nursery to find comparable substitutes.

Remember to keep your plants watered and your moss spritzed throughout the life of your indoor garden. Be careful not to add too much water…even though you have protected your table with plastic, it's still possible for water to overflow.

Snow Business

SWIRL ORNAMENTS

(shown on page 17)

Randomly reversing the direction of the swirls as you paint, use a liner paintbrush and white acrylic paint to create white swirls on a 2" diameter shiny blue glass ball ornament. Sprinkle iridescent glitter onto the ornament while the paint is wet, then shake off the excess and allow it to dry.

SNOW-CAPPED ORNAMENTS

(shown on page 17)

To create the snowy caps on each of these festive ornaments, use a stencil brush or craft stick to apply a thick coat of textured snow medium to the top of a red teardrop-shaped glass ornament. Sprinkle iridescent glitter onto the ornament while the medium is wet, then shake off the excess and allow to it to dry.

FELT STARS

(shown on pages 16 and 17)

You will need tracing paper, felt (we used yellow, dark yellow, light green and green), pinking sheers (if needed), embroidery floss (we used yellow, red, and blue), and polyester fiberfill.

1. For each star, trace desired star pattern, page 170, onto tracing paper; cut out. Use pattern to cut two stars from felt. (For star D, cut out using pinking sheers.)

2. Matching edges and leaving an opening for stuffing, use six strands of floss and work *Running Stitches*, page 183, to sew stars together; stuff with fiberfill and stitch opening closed.

3. To make stars into ornaments, run a length of floss through top back of one point and knot ends together to make a hanger.

SNOWMAN ORNAMENTS

(shown on page 17)

You will need tracing paper, white polyester fleece, orange and black embroidery floss, polyester fiberfill, assorted colors of felt, heavy-duty thread, assorted clear or white buttons, and clear nylon thread.

Refer to Embroidery Stitches, page 182 before beginning project. Use a 1/2" seam allowance for all sewing.

1. Trace snowman A pattern, page 168, onto tracing paper; cut out. Use pattern to cut two snowman shapes from fleece.

2. Using six strands of floss, work orange *Straight Stitches* for nose on one snowman shape (front); work black *Straight Stitches* for mouth, and black *French Knots* for eyes and buttons.

3. For each arm, cut a 3/4" x 3 1/2" strip from fleece; knot one end. Referring to Fig. 1, match unknotted end of each arm to edges on right side of front snowman shape and tack in place.

Fig. 1

Tips

To hold and steady your ornaments while painting and allowing them to dry, use a cup or mug with an opening slightly smaller than the diameter of the ornament.

Use an assembly-line method when working on multiples, like ball ornaments. The ones you started first should be dry and ready to move on to the second step by the time you finish the first step on the last ornament.

4. With arms to inside, matching right sides, and leaving an opening at the bottom for turning and stuffing, sew snowman shapes together. Turn right side out and stuff lightly with fiberfill; sew opening closed.

5. For scarf, cut a $\frac{1}{2}$" x 7" strip from felt; cut fringe in ends of felt strip. Tie scarf around snowman's neck.

6. For hat, cut a $2\frac{1}{2}$" x $4\frac{1}{2}$" piece from felt; turn one long edge up $\frac{1}{2}$" for cuff. Matching right sides, sew short edges together. Use heavy thread and work *Running Stitches* along top edge of hat, then pull stitches to gather; knot and trim ends. Turn hat right side out. If desired, sew buttons to hat, with seam at back. Place hat on snowman and tack in place.

7. For hanger, run a length of nylon thread through top back of ornament; knot ends together to form a loop.

SNOW SCENE PILLOW

(shown on page 19)

You will need tracing paper; white polyester fleece; orange and black embroidery floss; polyester fiberfill; brown and other colors of felt; heavy-duty thread; buttons for hat; two $\frac{1}{4}$" dia. green pom-poms; fabric glue; white jumbo rickrack; 12" x 14" piece of blue felt for panel background; $2\frac{1}{2}$" x 14" piece of cream fleece; three Felt Stars made with A, B, and C star patterns (without hangers, page 170); $\frac{1}{8}$" dia. white pom-poms; star buttons for panel; two 19" x 23" pieces of red felt for pillow front and back; and $2\frac{1}{3}$ yds. 1" dia. white ball fringe.

Use a $\frac{1}{2}$" seam allowance for all sewing. Allow glue to dry after each application; if necessary, hold items in place with clothespins or straight pins until dry.

1. For snowmen, follow Steps 1 – 6 of Snowman Ornaments instructions, page 142, using snowman B and C patterns, pages 168 and 169, and using a $\frac{3}{4}$" x 4" felt strip for each arm and a $\frac{3}{4}$" x 7" felt strip for each scarf, and making a hat for snowman B. Glue green pom-poms to snowman C for earmuffs.

2. For tree, trace trunk pattern, page 169, onto tracing paper; cut out. Use pattern to cut trunk from brown felt.

3. Mitering corners, glue rickrack along edges on back of panel background.

4. Cut curves along one long edge of cream fleece to resemble a snowbank, then glue to background. Glue snowmen, then tree trunk and Felt Stars to background. Glue white pom-poms to background randomly for falling snow; sew star buttons in place.

5. To assemble pillow, center and glue panel on right side of pillow front. Baste fringe along edges on right side of pillow front piece. Matching right sides and leaving an opening for turning and stuffing, sew pillow front and back together. Clip corners, then turn right side out. Stuff pillow with fiberfill; sew opening closed.

SNOWY TREE SKIRT

(shown on page 19)

You will need $1\frac{2}{3}$ yds. red felt; string; removable fabric marking pen; thumbtack; three Snow Scene Pillow panels (Steps 1 – 4, this page); fabric glue; 6 yds. white ball fringe; and 1" dia. white pom-poms.

Use a $\frac{1}{2}$" seam allowance for all sewing. Allow glue to dry after each application; if necessary, hold items in place with clothespins or straight pins until dry.

1. For skirt, fold felt in half from top to bottom and again from left to right. Tie one end of string to pen.

2. For outer cutting line, insert thumbtack through string 30" from pen; insert thumbtack through folded corner of felt as shown in Fig. 1; draw outer cutting line. For inner cutting line, reinsert thumbtack through string 2" from pen; insert thumbtack through folded corner and draw inner cutting line.

Fig. 1

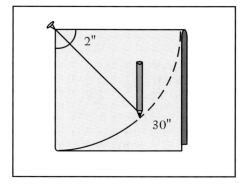

3. Cut out skirt through all layers, along drawn lines. For opening in back of skirt, cut through one layer along one folded edge from outer to inner edge.

4. Evenly space Snow Scene Pillow panels on skirt and glue in place. Glue fringe along outer edge of skirt, then glue 1" dia. pom-poms randomly on skirt for falling snow.

Tip

Let the kids help – have them glue on the pom-pom snowflakes!

SNOWMAN TREE TOPPER

(shown on page 15)

You will need string; pencil; thumbtack; 13" square of poster board; hot glue gun; high-loft batting; white polyester fleece; 28" of ¼"w satin ribbon; white heavy-duty thread; black embroidery floss; black, orange, and red felt; fabric glue; ⅜" dia. black buttons; tracing paper; polyester fiberfill; ice pick; two 20"-long pieces of 18-gauge floral wire; needle-nose pliers; 1½" x 24" strip of felt for scarf; and a Felt Star made with star D pattern (without hanger, page 142).

Refer to Embroidery Stitches, page 182, before beginning project. Use a ½" seam allowance for all sewing. Use fabric glue for all gluing unless otherwise indicated; allow glue to dry after each application.

1. To make base, tie one end of string around pencil; insert thumbtack through string 13" from pencil. Insert thumbtack through one corner of poster board as shown in Fig. 1 and draw cutting line. Cut out base.

Fig. 1

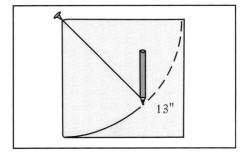

2. Forming a cone and overlapping edges ½", hot glue straight edges of base together. Glue a piece of batting around base, trimming to fit.

3. Enlarge snowman body pattern, page 171, 200%. Fold a 26" square of fleece in half. Placing pattern on fold as indicated, cut body from fleece.

4. Matching right sides, fold body in half lengthwise and sew straight edges together. For casing, press bottom edge of body ¾" to wrong side; sew casing closed. Make a small opening in casing to insert ribbon; thread ribbon through casing (Fig. 2). Turn body right side out.

Fig. 2

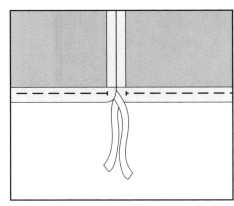

5. Use heavy-duty thread and work *Running Stitches* around body ¼" and 5" from top edge. With seam at back, mark placement for mouth, eyes, and nose between stitching lines. For mouth, use black floss to work *Backstitches* with *French Knots* at the corners and center. For eyes, cut two ½" dia. circles from black felt and glue to face. Sew buttons to front of snowman.

6. For nose, trace nose pattern, page 171, onto tracing paper; cut out. Use pattern to cut nose from orange felt. Fold nose in half lengthwise and sew straight edges together. Turn right side out and stuff with fiberfill. Work *Running Stitches* around nose ¼" from open end; pull stitches to gather, then fold gathers to center, making a flat base. Glue nose, seam side down, to face.

7. With seam at back, place body over base; pull casing ribbon to gather bottom of fleece under base, then knot and trim ends.

8. To shape snowman head, pull thread at neck to gather stitches against base; knot and trim thread ends. Stuff head with fiberfill, then pull thread at top to gather fabric; knot and trim thread ends.

9. Use ice pick to punch a hole through body 1½" below neck on each side of body for arms.

10. For each arm, curl one end of wire into a small loop. Cut a 3" x 8½" piece from fleece. Leaving 3" of fleece unglued at one end, hot glue wire to one long edge of fleece (Fig. 3); roll fleece over wire and hot glue edge to secure. For hand, knot fleece at end of wire loop; trim fleece to 1" past knot.

Fig. 3

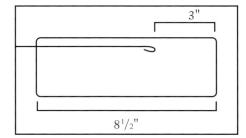

11. Insert wire end through hole in body. On inside, bend wire into a long, narrow U and hot glue to base to hold arm position in place (Fig. 4). Hot glue arm to body.

Fig. 4

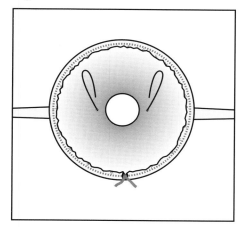

12. For hat, cut a 9" x 15" piece from red felt. Matching right sides, sew short edges together; turn right side out. Cut 2"-long strips for fringe every ¼" along top edge of hat. Use heavy-duty thread and work *Running Stitches* just below fringe; pull thread tight and knot to secure. Turn up cuff ½", then 2"; press. Place hat on head and tack in place.

13. For scarf, cut fringe in ends of felt strip; tie scarf around snowman's neck. Sew star to hand.

Tip

Our Snowman Gift Holders are the perfect stocking substitutes! These festive folk have pockets for holding Christmas candies and little gifts. Make one for each person in the family!

SNOWMAN GIFT HOLDERS
(shown on page 18)

For each holder, you will need white polyester fleece, corrugated cardboard, utility scissors, buttons, black embroidery floss, fabric glue, white rickrack, polyester fiberfill, tracing paper, orange and other colors felt, heavy-duty thread, and 1¾" dia. green pom-poms.

Refer to Embroidery Stitches, page 182, before beginning project. Use a ½" seam allowance for all sewing.

1. For each holder, enlarge snowman holder pattern D or E with matching pocket and base patterns, pages 172 through 174, 125%; cut out. Follow *Making Patterns*, page 180, to make whole patterns. Use patterns to cut two snowman pieces, a pocket, and a base from fleece. Draw around base pattern on cardboard; cut out base ½" inside drawn line.

2. Mark placement for eyes, nose, and mouth on one snowman shape (front); sew on buttons for eyes. For mouth, use six strands of floss to work *Backstitches* with *French Knots* at corners and center.

3. Hem top edge of pocket ¼" to wrong side; glue rickrack over hemline on right side of pocket. Sew buttons to pocket. Baste pocket onto right side of front snowman piece.

4. For each arm, cut a 1½" x 9" strip from fleece; knot one end. Referring to Fig. 1, match unknotted end of each arm to edges on right side of front snowman shape and tack in place.

Fig. 1

5. With arms to the inside, leaving bottom open, matching right sides, and referring to start and stop indicators on pattern, sew snowman pieces together; make a clip in seam allowance at start and stop points. Matching edges, pin fleece base to bottom of snowman; leaving one end of base open for turning, stuffing, and inserting cardboard base, sew pieces together. Turn snowman right side out, stuff with fiberfill, then insert cardboard base; sew opening closed.

6. For nose, follow Step 6 of Snowman Tree Topper, page 144, to make and attach nose.

7. For scarf, cut a 1¼" x 24" strip from felt; cut fringe in each end. Tie scarf around snowman's neck.

8. For hat for snowman D, use a 5" x 9" felt strip and follow Step 6 of Snowman Ornaments instructions, page 142.

9. For earmuffs on snowman E, glue pom-poms to head.

CANDLE CENTERPIECE
(shown on page 21)

You will need a hot glue gun, plastic foam floral disk to fit in basket of candleholder, wire basket candleholder (ours has wire loops under each candlecup), preserved salal leaves, artificial artichoke spray, green artificial berry spray, preserved cream hydrangea, reindeer moss, needle-nose pliers, 20-gauge gold craft wire, assorted glass beads, and candles.

1. Glue foam disk in basket. Arrange and glue leaves around edge of foam to cover; trim bottom edges of leaves if necessary.

2. Arrange artichoke and berry sprays, securing stems in foam. Fill in with hydrangea and moss.

3. For each beaded dangle, curl one end of a 3" length of wire into a tight loop. Thread beads onto wire, then curl remaining end to make a hanging loop. Hang dangles on wire loops below each candlecup; place candles in cups.

MATTELASSÉ RUNNER
(shown on page 21)

You will need a 15" x 32" piece each of muslin and mattelassé fabric, 3 yds. each of 1"w satin ribbon and cream trim, and clear nylon thread.

1. Matching right sides and leaving an opening for turning, use a ¹/₂" seam allowance to sew muslin and mattelassé pieces together. Clip corners and turn right side out; press. Sew opening closed.

2. Mitering at corners, pin ribbon, then trim, along edges of runner. Use nylon thread and a zigzag stitch to secure in place.

IVORY DECAL ORNAMENTS
(shown on page 22)

For each ornament, you will need a matte finish ivory glass ornament (ours measure 3¹/₂" dia.), Lazertran transfer paper, and a gold paint pen.

1. Enlarge or reduce desired botanical print from pages 148, 149, and 150 to fit on ornament; copy print onto transfer paper.

2. Follow manufacturer's instructions to transfer image onto ornament.

3. Use pen to paint dots on ornament.

PRETTY PLATES
(shown on page 23)

You will need white pierced-edge plates (our ornament plates measure 3⁷/₈" x 5¹/₂" and 4" x 5³/₈" and our larger plates measure 6" dia., 8³/₄" dia., and 9¹/₂" dia.), Lazertran transfer paper, gold paint pen, and ¹/₄"w sheer ribbon and ⁷/₈"w variegated wired ribbon (optional) to coordinate with botanical print.

1. Enlarge or reduce desired botanical print from pages 148, 149, and 150 to fit plate; copy print onto transfer paper.

2. Follow manufacturer's instructions to transfer print onto center of plate. Use pen to add decorative details to plate.

3. For hanger, weave ribbon through pierced areas along edge of plate or thread ribbon through holes at top of plate; tie into a bow.

BEADED PAPER TRIMS
(shown on page 22)

Make beautiful beaded paper ornaments using your favorite holiday paper punches, stickers, and beads.

For the ribbon ornaments, adhere punched shapes or stickers to 1¹/₂" dia. paper-punched circles, then embellish with beads.

For the medallion ornament, use a stylus to emboss a piece of vellum with the leaf pattern on page 175, cut it out just beyond the outer embossed lines and adhere it to the center of a 3" dia. paper-punched circle.

Refer to *Beading Basics*, page 184, to create beaded strands on sheer ribbon or wire. Attach embellished circles by gluing the wire or ribbon of the strand between the embellished circle and a plain circle, or cut a small slit in the top of the embellished circle and thread the ribbon through the opening. Attach the ends of the beaded strands to the loops of a jewelry finding and hang from an ornament hook.

EMBELLISHED PILLOWS
(shown on page 22)

Pillow with Flap
You will need two 11¹/₂" lengths each of 1"w crocheted trim and 1"w moss green satin ribbon to match table runner piece, fabric glue, 11"-long piece cut from the end of a lace-edged linen table scarf for flap (flap should be no wider than 14"), two 17" x 21" pieces of tapestry fabric, polyester fiberfill, and buttons.

Use a ¹/₂" seam allowance for all sewing.

1. Matching end of crocheted trim to cut edge of table runner piece, use fabric glue to attach trim pieces, then ribbon pieces along edges on wrong side of flap; glue ends of edgings to wrong side to finish.

2. Center and pin raw edge of flap along one long edge on right side of one fabric piece; baste in place. Matching right sides and leaving an opening for turning, sew fabric pieces together. Clip corners, then turn right side out. Stuff with fiberfill and sew opening closed.

3. Embellish flap with a ribbon bow and buttons as desired.

Mattelassé Pillow
You will need crocheted trim, two 1 yd. lengths of 3¹/₂"w green sheer wired ribbon, two 16" squares of mattelassé fabric, polyester fiberfill, and an upholstery-covered button.

Use a ¹/₂" seam allowance for all sewing.

1. Referring to Fig. 1, pin trim and ribbons on right side of one fabric piece. Tack trim to secure; baste ribbon ends in place.

Fig. 1

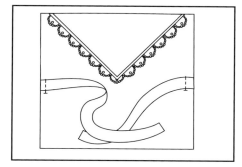

2. Matching right sides and leaving an opening for turning, sew fabric pieces together. Clip corners, then turn right side out. Stuff with fiberfill and sew opening closed.

3. Tie ribbon into a bow at front center; notch ends. Covering point of trim, sew button to center of bow.

Botanical Print Pillow Sleeve
You will need small purchased pillow (ours measures 11¹/₂" x 15¹/₂"), muslin, ³/₄"w crocheted trim, and photo transfer paper.

Use a ¹/₄" seam allowance for all sewing.

1. Loosely measure around center of pillow; add ¹/₂". Determine desired width of sleeve; add ¹/₂". Cut two strips of muslin the determined measurements.

2. Matching edges, baste a length of trim along each long edge of one muslin strip. Matching right sides, sew strips together along long edges; turn right side out and press.

3. Enlarging or reducing desired botanical print from pages 148, 149, and 150 to fit strip; copy print onto transfer paper.

4. Follow manufacturer's instructions to transfer print onto center of strip.

5. Matching right sides, sew ends of strip together. Press seam open and turn right side out. Place sleeve on pillow.

EMBROIDERED CHENILLE THROW
(shown on page 22)

You will need removable fabric marking pen, light green chenille throw, tear-away stabilizer, brown and green embroidery floss, 7mm variegated green embroidery ribbon, and 6mm light green variegated glass beads.

Refer to Embroidery Stitches, page 182, before beginning project. Use six strands of floss for all embroidery.

1. Use fabric marking pen to draw lines for main limb and branches on one edge of throw. Cut a piece of stabilizer larger than drawn design. Baste stabilizer to back of throw behind design.

2. Using brown floss, work *Satin Stitches* over the limb and *Backstitches* over the branches.

3. Use ribbon to make *Lazy Daisy Stitches* for leaves along branches. Use green floss to sew on beads for berries.

4. Follow manufacturers' instructions to remove stabilizer and any visible design marks.

BERRIED TOPIARIES
(shown on page 23)

Purchased berry-covered cones top decorative pots. Fill the pots with floral foam, then glue the cones to the foam. Gluing to secure, surround the small topiaries with reindeer moss and the large topiaries with moss and Masai pods ... wear gloves when handling the pods.

FRENCH COUNTRY VINEGAR BOTTLES

(shown on page 23)

For each bottle, you will need a corked decorative bottle filled with a flavored vinegar (see our recipe this page), crème wax, green and yellow-gold crayons, assorted crystal beads, beading needle and thread, craft glue, and a 20" length of $^1/_8$"w cream satin ribbon.

1. Cut cork even with bottle top. Follow manufacturer's instructions to melt wax; add crayons until desired color is achieved.

2. For seal, dip top of bottle into melted wax; turn bottle upright and allow wax to harden slightly. Repeat until desired thickness is achieved. If wax forms a cone shape, lightly press against a smooth surface to flatten. Allow wax to harden completely.

3. Referring to *Beading Basics*, page 184, and using *Locking Beads* at tops and bottoms of the bead sections, make three bead dangles on thread; leave extra thread at top of each dangle. Glue threads of dangles to center of ribbon; trim thread ends. Beginning at center of ribbon; wrap ribbon ends around neck of bottle. Knot ribbon at back of bottle and trim ends.

FRENCH COUNTRY VINEGARS

Look for the freshest varieties of produce to make flavored vinegars for giving.

> Sprigs of fresh herbs
> Pearl onions
> Garlic cloves
> Assorted variety of peppers
> White vinegar

Sterilize glass containers by washing in warm soapy water, rinsing, and immersing in boiling water for 10 minutes. Carefully invert containers to drain on a clean towel. Sterilize corks by dipping in boiling water with tongs several times. Fill with desired ingredients and hot vinegar while containers are warm.

Thoroughly wash herbs and vegetables; pat dry. Dip herbs in a sanitizing solution of 1 teaspoon household chlorine bleach mixed in 6 cups of water. Rinse thoroughly and pat dry. Lightly crush herbs. Cut small slits in onions, garlic cloves, and peppers. Place herbs and vegetables in sterilized glass containers. In a medium non-aluminum saucepan, bring vinegar almost to a boil over high heat; pour over ingredients. Insert corks; let stand in a cool place at least 10 days and up to 4 weeks for flavor to develop.

If herbs and vegetables lose their color during storage, follow the above instructions to prepare containers and fresh ingredients, then add strained flavored vinegar. Store in a cool place up to 3 months or refrigerator up to 6 months. Discard prepared vinegars if there are any signs of spoilage.

Leisure Arts, Inc., grants permission to the owner of this book to photocopy the pattern on this page for personal use only.

AMARYLLIS-COVERED CHRISTMAS DÉCOR
(shown on page 25)

Amaryllis-Covered Topiaries

For each topiary, you will need enough artificial amaryllis to cover cone, 36"h foam cone, T-pins, artificial red grape clusters, and assorted glass ball ornaments.

1. Remove amaryllis blossoms from stems, leaving enough stem to insert into foam; cover cone with amaryllis.

2. Use T-pins to attach grapes and ornaments to cone as desired.

Floral Wreath

You will need floral wire, wire cutters, 36" dia. floral foam wreath, and enough artificial amaryllis to cover wreath.

1. For hanger, wrap a length of wire around top of wreath; twist wire tightly around wreath, then forming a loop, twist wire ends together.

2. Remove amaryllis blossoms from stems, leaving enough stem to insert into foam; cover wreath with amaryllis.

Amaryllis Globes

For each globe, you will need enough artificial amaryllis to cover ball, floral foam ball (we used various large-size balls), and red ribbon and T-pins to make ornaments.

1. Remove amaryllis blossoms from stems, leaving enough stem to insert into foam; cover ball with amaryllis.

2. To hang ball as an ornament, cut a length of ribbon long enough to hang from ceiling; make a knot near both ends of ribbon. Using a T-pin, secure one knot in ribbon to the ball and the other end to the ceiling.

TABLETOP TREE
(shown on page 24)

You will need oversized and other assorted ornaments; artificial Christmas tree to fit on table; extra-wide wire-edged ribbon; artificial amaryllis, amaranthus, sunflowers, and berry stems; pheasant feathers; cymbidium orchids; and several Amaryllis Globes (this page).

1. Hang oversized ornaments on inner parts of branches. Tuck ribbon inside the branches as you wrap it around the tree. Hang additional ornaments on tree as desired.

2. Wiring in place as needed, arrange amaryllis, amaranthus, sunflowers, and berry stems in tree as desired.

3. For tree topper, interweave additional amaryllis blossoms in top of tree, then add pheasant feathers and orchid stems.

4. Add Amaryllis Globes and large ornaments at base of tree.

COLUMN SWAG
(shown on page 26)

You will need four heavy-duty hooks with adhesive backs (we used 3M™ Jumbo Hooks with Command™ Adhesive), chenille stems, four large caged floral foam blocks, craft glue, Spanish moss, artificial greenery, artificial amaryllis, ribbon, T-pins, and assorted ornaments.

1. Adhere a hook to each side of column; then, using chenille stems, hang a floral cage from each hook.

2. Use glue to cover foam with Spanish moss, then arrange greenery and amaryllis in foam as desired; allow to dry.

3. To hang each ornament from swag, cut desired length of ribbon; knot one end. Using a T-pin, attach knotted end of ribbon to foam. Thread remaining end through hanger on ornament and knot in place.

Tips

To add stability to floral arrangements, cover artificial floral stem ends in hot glue before inserting them into the foam; hold stem in place until the glue sets.

To save yourself time and money when creating a spectacular theme using one primary element, like our amaryllis, shop on the Internet or at wholesale floral suppliers and buy in bulk.

Cookies, Cookies, Everywhere!

Recipe Card, Invitation, and Envelope
(shown on page 30)

You will need green, white, and red card stock; red and white striped paper; green and black markers; craft glue stick; holly-motif and clear-backed red alphabet stickers (ours are $^{7}/_{16}$" dia.); star rubber stamp; red ink pad; 5" x 7" white cards with envelopes; colored pencils; and white pom-poms.

Recipe Cards

1. To make each recipe card, cut a $3^{1}/_{2}$" x 5" piece from green card stock and a $3^{1}/_{4}$" x $4^{3}/_{4}$" piece from white card stock.

2. Cut a $^{1}/_{2}$" x $4^{3}/_{4}$" piece from striped paper; glue along top edge of white card. Use green marker to draw evenly spaced lines across the card.

3. Adhere holly sticker to white card stock; cut out around design, then glue to top left corner of card.

4. Center and glue white card on green card.

Invitation

1. Stamp stars on front of card to within $^{3}/_{4}$" of outside long edges; stamp right half of inside of card.

2. Cut two $^{1}/_{2}$" x 7" strips from striped paper; glue strips $^{3}/_{8}$" inside long edges on front of card. Use green marker to draw two straight lines between striped paper and edges of card.

3. Using patterns on page 175, photocopy face and banner onto white card stock, hat and banner background onto red card stock, and mittens onto green card stock; cut out.

4. Use black marker to outline Santa pieces and features; use colored pencils to shade and color cheeks, nose, eyebrows, mustache, and beard. Arrange pieces on card and glue in place. Leaving center intact, cut one side off pom-pom; glue to hat.

5. Use stickers to spell out "Cookie Swap" on banner.

6. Photocopy inside invitation design, page 175, onto white paper; write in additional information. Cut out design just inside dashed line. Cut two $^{1}/_{2}$" x $3^{1}/_{2}$" strips from striped paper; glue along top and bottom edges of design.

7. Adhere two holly stickers to white card stock; cut out around designs, then glue one sticker to top left corner and one to bottom right corner of form.

8. Center and glue design inside card; place blank recipe cards inside invitation.

Envelope

1. With envelope open, stamp stars on flap. Fold flap down and draw green lines just below edges of flap.

2. Place invitation and recipe cards inside envelope and seal. Then glue a $^{1}/_{2}$" x $1^{1}/_{2}$" piece of striped paper over the point of the flap to secure. Adhere a holly sticker to center of striped paper.

Santa Pin
(shown on page 32)

For each pin, you will need tracing paper; stylus; white, red, and beige craft foam; $^{1}/_{4}$" dia. hole punch; craft glue; black permanent fine-point marker; 1"-long adhesive pinback; three 24" lengths of assorted narrow ribbon; $3^{3}/_{4}$" x 9" clear cellophane bag; and cookies to fill bag.

1. Trace Santa patterns, page 176, onto tracing paper. Use stylus to transfer hat brim, mustache, and beard patterns onto white foam, hat onto red foam, and face onto beige foam. Cut the pieces from foam.

2. Use hole punch to make a pom-pom from white foam for hat. Layer and glue foam pieces together. Use marker to draw details on Santa.

3. Adhere pinback to back of Santa. Thread ribbons through pinback, then tie around bag filled with cookies, making a bow behind pin.

Tip

When making your Invitation and Envelope, using a rubber stamp wheel with a star motif will make stamping the design fast and fun.

PLACE CARDS

(shown on page 31)

For each card, you will need red and green card stock, green checked paper, decorative-edge craft scissors, clear-backed holiday border stickers, clear-backed red alphabet stickers (ours are $^7/_{16}$" dia.) or red permanent fine-point marker, craft glue, and a Santa icing decoration.

1. Cut a $4^1/_2$" x $6^1/_2$" piece from red card stock and a $2^1/_4$" x $3^1/_2$" piece from green checked paper. Using craft scissors, cut a $2^3/_4$" x $3^7/_8$" piece from green card stock.

2. Adhere border sticker $^1/_4$" above bottom edge of checked piece; trim sticker edges even with paper. Use letter stickers or marker to spell out cookie name on center of checked piece.

3. Matching short edges, fold red paper piece in half. Center and glue checked paper piece to green paper piece, then green piece to front of red paper piece. Glue icing decoration to top of place card.

PAINTED MUG

(shown on page 35)

You will need a mug, rubbing alcohol, red and green porcelain glazes, paintbrushes, and clear-backed red alphabet stickers (ours are $^7/_{16}$" dia.).

1. Clean mug with alcohol.

2. Following manufacturer's instructions for using glazes, paint desired designs on mug, allowing room to place stickers. Bake mug to set paint.

3. When mug has cooled, apply stickers to mug (stickers will withstand several hand-washings; do not soak or wash mug in dishwasher).

Invitation and Envelope

Place Card

Recipe Card

WOODLAND WONDER

PINECONE ORNAMENTS

(shown on page 40)

Lightly paint the tips of a large pinecone with metallic gold paint and allow to dry. Arrange and glue artificial greenery and berries to the flat end of the pinecone.

To make a hanger, fold an 8" length of ⁵/₈"w red satin ribbon into a loop; hot glue the ends of the loop to the top of the ornament. Tie a 20" length of ribbon into a bow; trim ends. Hot glue the bow to the top of the ornament, covering the ends.

WOODBURNED ORNAMENTS

(shown on page 40)

For each ornament, you will need a wooden ornament (we used a 3¹/₂"h x 3¹/₂"dia. teardrop-shaped and a 2²/₃"h x 3¹/₂" dia. round ornament), fine-grit sandpaper, tack cloth, tracing paper, transfer or graphite paper, wood burning tool, metallic gold rub-on finish, and ¹/₂ yd. of red satin wire-edged ribbon.

1. Sand ornament with the grain, then wipe with tack cloth to remove dust.

2. Using a star pattern from page 176, follow *Transferring Patterns*, page 180 to transfer pattern onto ornament.

3. Follow woodburning tool manufacturer's instructions to lightly burn along transferred lines, then shade desired areas by burning along inside of lines at a slower pace.

4. Leaving burned area unfinished, apply gold finish to ornament, then buff to desired sheen.

5. Hang ornament from a ribbon bow.

APPLIQUÉD PILLOW

(shown on page 39)

You will need two 11" squares of muslin; red fabric for pillow front, borders, and pillow back; red fabric for bird body and wing; scraps of black, yellow, and brown fabrics for mask, beak, and branch; freezer paper; yellow, brown, red and green embroidery floss; 14" square pillow form; and eight 1¹/₄" to 1³/₄"-long twigs.

Refer to Embroidery Stitches, page 182, before beginning project. Refer to Pillow Stitching Diagram, page 155, and use three strands of floss for all embroidery unless otherwise indicated. Use a ¹/₂" seam allowance for all sewing unless otherwise indicated.

1. Baste muslin squares together.

2. Trace patterns, pages 176 and 177, onto matte side of freezer paper; cut out. Place patterns, shiny side down, on wrong side of fabric and use a warm iron to secure them in place. Cut out shapes ¹/₈" outside pattern edges. Using pattern edges as a guide and clipping fabric at curves as necessary, press seam allowance to wrong side; remove patterns from fabric.

3. Arrange and pin appliqués in place on muslin. Using a coordinating color of thread or one strand of floss, blind stitch appliqués in place.

4. Using a coordinating color of floss for each appliqué, work *Backstitches* along edges of appliqués to outline. Work *Backstitches* and *Straight Stitches* for feathers on wing and tail. Work *Backstitches* for legs and feet and for

definition of top notch, beak, and brow. Work long *Straight Stitches* for pine needles and *French Knots* for berries and eye.

5. Cut two 3" x 11" strips for side borders, two 3" x 15" strips for top and bottom borders, and a 15" square for pillow back from red fabric.

6. Sew side, then top and bottom borders to appliquéd muslin. Place pillow front and back right sides together. Leaving bottom edge open for turning, sew pieces together. Turn right side out; insert pillow form and sew opening closed.

7. Using six strands of red floss, tack two twigs at each corner of muslin piece; knot floss to secure.

CANDLE WREATH

(shown on page 41)

You will need a tall black metal candleholder (ours measures 11"h with a 5" dia. plate), Design Master® Glossy wood-tone spray, plastic foam disc to fit on candleholder plate, green sheet moss, greening pins, hot glue gun, fresh greenery, artificial berry garland, 1¹/₂"w red sheer wire-edged ribbon, and a candle.

1. Apply wood-tone spray to candleholder and allow to dry. Glue foam disc to top of candleholder. Cover foam with moss; pin to secure.

2. Insert sprigs of greenery and garland into and around foam, forming a wreath; pin as needed to secure. Weave ribbon through greenery; tie another length of ribbon into a bow and hot glue bow to front of wreath.

3. Place candle at center of wreath on candleholder.

WOODLAND GARLANDS

(shown on pages 38 – 41)

The charming garlands and floral arrangement above the mantel are made using the same basic technique.

First, weave sheer metallic wire-edged ribbon through a curly-branched berry garland. Use wire to attach gilded pinecones and grapevine star ornaments, redbirds, and satiny glass ball ornaments. Bows can accent the ends or create a center focal point. Lastly, intersperse fresh springs of traditional holiday greenery into the garland to add the distinctive aroma of Christmas.

Tips

Wire the ends of more than one garland together to create the appropriate length for the areas in which you are decorating. Cover up the junction with one of your pretty adornments.

Refer to *Bows*, page 185 to make *Multi-loop Bows* to add to your festive decorations.

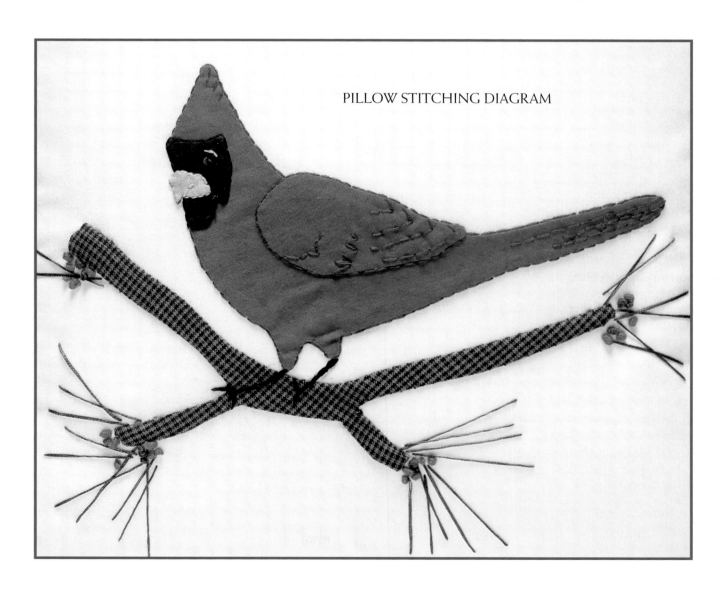

PILLOW STITCHING DIAGRAM

DECORATED BOTTLE ORNAMENTS AND LUMINARIES

(shown on pages 55 and 60)

You will need self-adhesive stickers (designs, borders, and alphabets); small clear plastic bottles for ornaments and large glass bottles for luminaries; floral spray paint and stain (we used bronze and gold paint and honey stain); craft knife; clear acrylic spray sealer; wire cutters; assorted gauges of craft wire (we used copper, gold, and antique gold); assorted beads; needle-nose pliers; hot glue gun; and candles to fit in large glass bottles.

1. For each ornament or luminary, adhere stickers to bottle as desired.

2. Spray paint bottle and allow to dry.

3. Use tip of craft knife to carefully remove stickers. Spray bottle with sealer and allow to dry.

4. For handle, wrap one end of one or two lengths of wire around threaded edge of bottle; twist wire around itself to secure. Thread beads onto wire as desired; twist wire or curl around a pencil to hold beads in place. Shape wire to form a handle, then secure wire end on opposite side of bottle; trim excess wire.

5. Thread beads onto a length of wire long enough to wrap around and cover threaded edge of bottle. Wrap beaded wire around edge of bottle; twist ends together to secure; trim excess wire.

6. For each beaded dangle, loop a length of wire around wire on bottle. Thread beads onto wire as desired; use a *Locking Bead*, page 184, to secure. Wrap wire around itself just above *Locking Bead*, then trim excess wire.

7. For each luminary, hot glue candle inside bottle.

FEATHER TASSELS

(shown on pages 55 and 58)

You will need primer, assorted wooden pieces to form tassel topper (for candle cup tassel we used a $1^3/_4$"h x $1^1/_4$"dia. candle cup with hole in bottom, $5/_8$" dia. wheel, and a $5/_8$" dia. half bead; for bell cup tassel we used a 2"h x $2^1/_4$" dia. bell cup with hole in bottom and a $3/_4$"h x $3/_4$"w bead), antique copper and antique gold metallic paint, paintbrushes, hot glue gun, natural sponge, feather garland (one package for each tassel; we used peacock and assorted tail and saddle hackle feathers), thin gold cord, liquid fray preventative, and glass beads.

Allow primer and paint to dry after each application. When applying hot glue to attach wooden pieces, be careful not to glue holes shut.

1. Prime, then paint a copper basecoat on wooden pieces.

2. Aligning the holes in each piece, glue desired wooden pieces to top of cup or bell to form tassel topper.

3. Using a mixture of one part gold paint and one part water, lightly *Sponge Paint* ornament (page 182).

4. Lay garland, wrong side up, on a flat surface. Glue one end of a 12" length of cord to end of garland. Dabbing hot glue on quills to secure as you go, roll feathers into a tassel. Trim quills evenly.

Tip

When making the Painted Glass Ball Ornaments, page 157, if you are unable to find corks to fit into your ornaments, hold the ornaments by the top when painting. Then, simply insert the skewers into the ornaments and into the plastic foam to allow it to dry. Replacing the caps will cover the unpainted tops.

5. Securing tassel in topper, thread remaining end of cord up through topper, then through two glass beads; knot cord above beads. Fold remaining cord in half, then tie an overhand loop knot (Figs. 1 and 2). Apply fray preventative to knot, allow to dry, then trim excess cord.

Fig. 1	Fig. 2
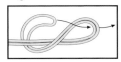	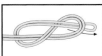

FINIAL ORNAMENTS

(shown on page 55)

For each ornament, you will need spray primer, an $4^1/_2$"h x 2" dia. unfinished wooden finial, antique copper and gold metallic paint, paintbrushes, natural sponge, hot glue gun, small gold cord, craft feathers (we used saddle hackle feathers), wooden doll pin stand, glass beads, and elastic thread.

Allow primer and paint to dry after each application.

1. Prime, then paint a copper basecoat on finial. *Sponge Paint*, page 182, upper and lower sections of finial with gold paint. Using a small paintbrush, paint gold vertical stripes around center of finial.

2. For hanger, knot together the ends of a length of cord, then glue knot at center of finial base.

3. Glue feathers around the outside of up-turned doll pin stand. Insert hanger up through center of doll pin stand; glue stand inside base of finial.

4. String beads on elastic thread; tie around base of feathers and glue in place.

EUCALYPTUS ORNAMENTS

(shown on page 54)

For each ornament, you will need gold seed beads, gold sequin pins, brown eucalyptus leaves, 4" dia. plastic foam ball, ribbon, and clear nylon thread.

1. Place one pin through a bead and insert through top center of each leaf. Starting at bottom of ball and working in layers, pin leaves around ball.

2. Tie a length of ribbon into a bow; attach to the top of the ornament with a pin.

3. For hanger, knot ends of a loop of thread and attach to the ornament with a pin.

PAINTED GLASS BALL ORNAMENTS

(shown on page 54)

For each ornament, you will need a clear glass ball ornament with removable cap; cork to fit inside opening of ornament; skewer; deep plastic bowl (larger than ornaments); gold, copper, and bronze spray paint; paper towels; and plastic foam to hold ornaments while drying.

1. Remove cap from ornament. Place cork on skewer, then insert cork into opening of ornament.

2. Fill bowl two-thirds full with water. Spray gold, copper, and/or bronze paint onto surface of water.

3. Dip ornament into paint mixture, covering it completely; blot dry with paper towel. Spray surface of water before dipping ornament each time. Repeat process until desired coverage is achieved.

4. Insert other end of skewer into plastic foam and allow ornament to dry. Spray ornament with sealer and allow to dry.

5. Remove cork and replace cap.

PAINT-SWIRLED GLASS BALL ORNAMENTS

(shown on page 54)

For each ornament, you will need a clear glass ball ornament with removable cap; metallic bronze, gold, and antique gold paint; hot glue gun; gold braid; and gold cord.

1. Remove cap from ornament; rinse inside of ornament with water.

2. Place $1/8$ to $1/4$ tsp water and one color of paint inside ornament. Swirl mixture until most of inside is covered. Pour out excess mixture and repeat with next color of paint.

3. Rotate ornament as it dries, pouring out excess mixture. Replace cap.

4. Glue braid around cap. For hanger, tie cord to a loop on cap.

ELEGANT BOXES

(shown on page 58)

For each box, you will need wood glue, metallic bronze and antique gold acrylic paint, paintbrushes, and gold faceted acrylic gems.

Refer to Dry Brush, page 181 before beginning projects. Allow glue and paint to dry after each application.

Chest

You will need unfinished wooden oval cutouts, papier-mâché chest, wooden buttons, and a decorative wooden accent piece.

1. Glue ovals along front and sides of top edge of lid. Glue buttons along sides and front of bottom edge of lid and on each side of top of lid. Glue decorative accent to front center on top of lid.

2. Paint box with two coats of bronze paint, then *Dry Brush* with gold paint.

3. Glue gems to center of ovals.

Round Box

You will need unfinished wooden circle cutouts, round papier-mâché box with lid, wooden buttons, wooden toy wheel, and four acorn dowel caps.

1. Glue circles along side of lid. Glue buttons along top edge of lid.

2. Paint box with two coats of bronze paint, then *Dry Brush* with gold paint.

3. Paint wheel, dowel caps, and one button with two coats of gold paint.

4. For finial, glue wheel to top center of lid; glue one dowel cap to top of wheel, then glue a button to top of dowel cap.

5. For legs, glue remaining dowel caps to bottom of box.

6. Glue gems to center of circles.

Small Rectangular Box

You will need three unfinished decorative wooden squares, papier-mâché box with lid, unfinished wooden square cutouts, and four ball finials.

1. Glue decorative squares to top of lid.

2. Paint lid and square cutouts with two coats of bronze paint, then *Dry Brush* with gold paint.

3. For legs, glue a finial to each bottom corner of box.

4. Paint box and legs with two coats of gold paint.

5. Arranging square cutouts "on-point," glue them along bottom edges of box.

6. Glue gems to centers of squares.

Tips

Any combination of unfinished wooden cutouts and acrylic jewels can transform a plain papier-mâché box into a decorative treasure chest. Be creative — use your imagination to create ornamental boxes of your own with different shapes!

If you are unable to find papier-mâché boxes with decorative patterns on the sides like ours, cover your boxes with textured wall paper before painting.

REINDEER PLACEMATS
(shown on pages 68 and 69)

For each placemat, you will need craft glue, two 6" x 12" pieces of green card stock, 12" square of red card stock, 11" square of white copier paper, medium-point black permanent marker, colored pencils, and 1/2" dia. tinsel pom-poms.

Allow glue to dry after each application.

1. For placemat, glue green card stock pieces to back of red card stock, leaving 3" of each green piece extending past sides of red the card stock.

2. Leaving room for child's "hand" antlers, trace reindeer pattern, page 178, onto 11" paper piece; glue reindeer to placemat.

3. Have child use marker to draw around each hand to form antlers on the reindeer, then color the reindeer and borders; add the name and year. Glue pom-poms to placemat.

"HANDY" GIFT TAGS
(shown on pages 68 and 70)

What fun! Colorful handprint tags add a personal touch to packages for everyone on your gift list. And they're so easy – the whole family can make them!

Draw around your hand onto colorful paper (like scrapbooking paper or craft paper) and cut out. Cut a rectangle from coordinating paper to make a cuff for a boy's hand. Glue on tinsel pom-poms for rings or a bracelet on a girl's hand.

If you'd like, make a hole for the hanger near the cuff or bracelet and thread embroidery floss through it, tying the ends into a knot to hang from the present. Don't forget to write the "to" and "from" information on the tag before attaching it to your gift!

MINIATURE HAND ORNAMENTS
(shown on page 70)

For each ornament, you will need a fine-point permanent marker, shrinkable plastic, colored pencils and markers, utility scissors, 1/4" dia. hole punch, 24-guage gold craft wire, wire cutters, and assorted red and green beads.

Read shrinkable plastic manufacturer's instructions before beginning project.

1. Have child use marker to draw around their hand onto plastic, then decorate plastic with colored pencils and markers.

2. Cut out shape, then punch a hole through shape for hanging.

3. Bake plastic shape and allow to cool.

4. To hang ornament, run one end of a length of wire through hole in ornament and twist end tightly around itself to secure. Thread beads onto wire. Form a loop in the end of the wire, then twist the wire around itself to secure; trim excess wire.

PHOTO ORNAMENTS
(shown on page 68)

You will need decorative papers (scrapbooking paper, card stock, craft paper, etc.), craft glue, photographs to fit on ornament, hole punch, embroidery floss, ribbon, small tinsel pom-poms, and a white colored pencil.

1. For the ornament, cut a circle or a rectangle from decorative paper. Cut strips of paper for the "ribbons." Arrange and glue the photo and "ribbons" on the ornament.

2. For the hanger, punch a hole at the top of the ornament, then thread a length of floss through the hole and knot ends together.

3. Tie a length of ribbon into a bow and glue to the top of the ornament; glue a pom-pom to center of the bow.

4. Use the colored pencil to write the name and date on the ornament.

Tip

Use an Izone™ camera to capture the moments of the day! The small, instant photographs make ideal pictures to use for these family ornaments. To add the non-adhesive backed photos, use a craft knife and cutting mat to make slits to hold the photo at the center of the ornament; slide the photo in place. If desired, cut another piece of card stock and glue it to the back of the ornament to hide the edges of the photo.

CRAFTY CREATIONS TO SHARE

BOTTLE SLEEVES AND TAGS
(shown on page 76)

For each sleeve, you will need green and red 11" x 17" corrugated kraft paper, unchilled bottled beverage, hot glue gun, red wire-edged ribbon, star stickers, white speckled card stock, Christmas tree and holiday greeting rubber stamps, green ink pad, green marker, craft glue, decorative-edge craft scissors, hole punch, hole reinforcements, red tissue paper, and green raffia.

1. For sleeve, cut a piece of green paper to fit loosely around body of bottle. Overlapping and hot gluing ends together at back, wrap paper around bottle.

2. Wrap a piece of ribbon around center of sleeve, hot gluing ends of ribbon to back of sleeve. Adhere stickers to ribbon. Remove bottle from sleeve.

3. For tag, cut a piece from card stock that is large enough to accommodate stamps (our measures $2^5/8$" x $4^1/2$"). Stamp tree on tag; color tree with marker and place a star sticker at top. Stamp greeting above tree. Randomly adhere extra stickers to tag. Use craft glue to adhere tag to red paper and allow to dry. Use craft scissors to cut paper $1/8$" outside edges of card stock. Punch a hole in top of tag; place hole reinforcement over hole.

4. Wrap tissue around bottle and place in sleeve. To hang tag, make a loop in raffia to fit loosely around bottle neck; knot at bottom of loop. Thread raffia through hole in tag and tie into a bow.

CHARM PIN GREETING CARDS AND ENVELOPES
(shown on page 77)

For each card, you will need assorted colors of paint for metal surfaces, paintbrushes, silicone adhesive, clothespin, pinback, card stock, and spray adhesive.

Cat Pin
You will need a cat charm (ours measures 1"w x $2^1/2$"h), decorative-edge craft scissors, red decorative paper, embellishing trim (we used assorted decorative yarns), holiday greeting rubber stamp, and a red ink pad.

1. Paint charm as desired; allow to dry.

2. Using silicone adhesive, attach pinback to back of charm; use clothespin to apply pressure until adhesive is completely dry.

3. For card, cut a piece of card stock larger than pin; fold in half. Stamp greeting on inside of card. Use craft scissors to cut a piece of red paper $1/4$" smaller on all sides than front of card. Using spray adhesive, glue red paper to front of card. Wrap trim around fold of card; knot on outside front, leaving streamers.

4. Cut two X's through front of card, where the distance apart is equal to the length of the pinback. With charm at front of card, insert pin through X's and close the clasp.

5. For envelope, enlarge or reduce pattern, page 179, until both length and width are at least $3/4$" larger than that of the card; cut out. Draw around pattern on card stock; cut out.

6. Fold envelope sides, then bottom as indicated on pattern and glue in place; insert card and fold top closed.

Bee Pin
You will need a bee charm (ours measures $2^1/8$"w x $1^1/2$"h), white flocked ribbon and iridescent mesh ribbon at least $3/8$" wider than pin, fabric glue, holiday greeting rubber stamp, silver ink pad, $1/4$"w sheer green ribbon, liquid fray preventative, artificial miniature greenery sprig with berries, and tiny white pearl buttons.

1. Follow Steps 1 and 2 of Cat Pin to make pin.

2. For card, cut a piece of card stock larger than pin. Spray card stock with adhesive, then cover with flocked ribbon; trim to fit. Spray mesh ribbon with adhesive and glue over ribbon covering front of card; trim ribbon edges even with card.

3. Follow Step 4 of Cat Pin to attach pin to card.

4. For envelope, measure longest side of card; double the measurement and add 2". Cut a length of flocked ribbon the determined measurement; trim one end to a point. Fold opposite end up to form a pocket; sew or glue edges to secure. Stamp greeting near bottom of envelope.

5. Cut a length of sheer ribbon slightly longer than width of pocket; apply fray preventative to ends. Sew greenery to ribbon. Using a small amount of fabric glue, secure ends of ribbon to front near top of envelope and allow to dry; sew buttons over ends of ribbon. Insert card, then tuck flap under sheer ribbon.

(Charm Pins continued on page 160)

Charm Pins continued from page 159

Bear Pin

You will need a bear charm (ours measures 1¼"w x 1⅝"h), small brown paper tag envelope, scrapbook border sticker, decorative vellum, black permanent fine-point marker, scrapbooking paper, and clear-backed alphabet stickers.

1. Follow Steps 1 and 2 of Cat Pin, page 159, to make pin.

2. For card, cut a piece of card stock to fit inside envelope. Leaving ¼" on all sides of card stock bare, adhere pieces of border to top and bottom of card. Cut a piece of vellum to fit between borders; use spray adhesive to attach to envelope.

3. Follow Step 4 of Cat Pin, page 159, to attach pin to card. Use marker to write message on card.

4. For envelope, cut a piece of vellum ⅛" smaller on all sides than front of tag envelope. Cut a piece of scrapbook paper ⅛" smaller on all sides than vellum. Using spray adhesive, glue vellum to center front of bag, then paper to center of vellum.

5. Use stickers to add a message on front of envelope.

GIFT BOXES AND TAG ORNAMENTS

(shown on page 78)

For each box, you will need red handmade paper, small folding gift box with handle, craft glue, white and green card stock, 2½"w silver wire-edged mesh ribbon, silver fine-point paint pen, ⅛" dia. hole punch, gift to place inside box, and narrow silver ribbon.

1. Tear a piece of handmade paper slightly smaller than front of box and glue in place.

2. For tag, cut a 2½" x 4" piece from white card stock and round the edges. Tear a piece from handmade paper slightly smaller than tag; glue to center of tag. Cut a small piece from mesh ribbon and trim the wire edges off; glue over handmade paper.

3. Draw a small Christmas tree on green card stock; embellish tree with silver pen. Cut out tree and glue to ribbon on tag. Punch a hole in top of tag.

4. Fill and close box. Wrap a length of mesh ribbon around front and back of box. Thread one end under handle and gather both ends at top of box. Tie a length of narrow ribbon into a bow around gathered ribbon ends. Cut a notch in each end of mesh ribbon.

5. Attach tag to box with narrow ribbon.

BOTTLED BATH SALTS AND GIFT TAGS

(shown on page 79)

For each container, you will need a small glass bottle with a cork stopper (ours measures 1¾" square by 4"h), bath salts, crème wax, cream perle cotton, white decorative yarn, beading needle and thread, small beads (we used pearl and gold), large silver heart bead, clear cellophane, decorative-edge craft scissors, handmade paper, card stock, craft glue, holiday greeting rubber stamp, silver ink pad, clear embossing powder, heat tool, ⅛" dia. hole punch, and a small silver bead.

Refer to Beading Basics, page 184, before beginning project.

1. Fill bottle with bath salts and cap with cork. Follow manufacturer's instructions to melt wax. For seal, dip top of bottle into melted wax, turning bottle upright and allowing wax to dry briefly after each dip, until desired thickness is achieved (we dipped ours seven to ten times). If wax forms a cone shape, lightly press top of wax against bottom of wax container to flatten. Allow wax to harden completely.

2. To decorate bottle, tie two strands each of perle cotton and decorative yarn around neck of bottle.

3. Referring to Fig. 1, and using a *Locking Bead*, thread a section of beads about two-thirds the height of bottle, then go up through heart bead with the thread and continue to thread enough beads to hang loosely around bottle neck. Push thread back through heart bead and continue to thread beads below heart. Use a *Locking Bead* to secure last bead in place, then *Secure Thread Ends*. Thread another strand of beads between the first two. Knot and trim thread.

Fig. 1

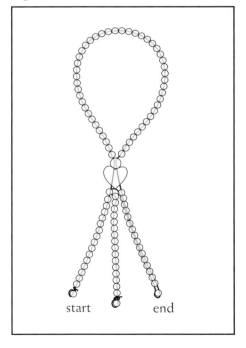

start   end

4. Wrap bottle in cellophane and tie with several strands of decorative yarn.

5. For tag, use craft scissors to cut a piece of card stock; cut a piece of handmade paper ¼" smaller on all sides. Glue smaller piece in center of larger piece. Stamp greeting on tag. While ink is still wet, dust stamped area with embossing powder, then follow heat tool manufacturer's instructions to emboss greeting.

6. Adding the small silver bead and other beads as desired, use decorative yarn to attach tag around cellophane.

HANDMADE SOAPS

(shown on page 80)

You will need glycerin soap blocks, soap colorant, additives (we used dried crumbled orange peel, whole oatmeal, an artificial fern frond, and a dried orange slice), soap molds, decorative-edge craft scissors, card stock, craft crimper (for paper and lightweight metal), hot glue gun, ³⁄₈"w gold wire-edged mesh ribbon, decorative shredded paper or wood excelsior, gift containers (we used a rectangular metal flower box and small and large hexagonal paper boxes), and clear glass candle dishes to fit inside gift containers (optional).

Bulk Additives

1. Follow manufacturer's instructions for melting soap blocks; add colorants. While soap is in a liquid state, stir in desired additives. Pour into molds and allow to cool.

2. Using craft scissors, cut ³⁄₄"w strips of card stock; run strips through crimper. Wrap strips around soaps; trim excess and glue ends together.

3. Wrap a length of ribbon around paper and soap; tie into a bow.

4. Put shredded paper or wood excelsior in container; place soaps on top. If desired, place soap on candle dish.

Single Additives

1. Follow manufacturer's instructions for melting soap blocks; add colorants.

2. Pour ¹⁄₈" thickness of soap into mold; allow to cool slightly, then gently press in additive. Cool almost completely. If necessary, reheat remaining soap and fill remainder of mold.

3. Follow Steps 2 – 4 of Bulk Additives.

ROSE PETAL SACHETS

(shown on page 81)

For each sachet, you will need a sheer sachet bag with drawstring handles, 1³⁄₈"w gold-edged sheer ribbon, craft glue, alphabet stickers, and scented rose petals.

1. Measure width of bag and add 1". Cut a length of ribbon the determined measurement.

2. Using craft glue and stickers, center and adhere a name or initials on ribbon.

3. Turn bag inside out and open seams on both sides. Arrange ribbon on center front of bag (inside bag); insert ends of ribbon into opened seams and resew seams. Trim excess ribbon. Turn bag right side out and fill with petals.

FLOWERPOT CANDLES

(shown on page 81)

For each candle, you will need ivory acrylic paint; paintbrush; small terra-cotta flowerpot (ours measure approx. 2³⁄₄"h x 2¹⁄₂" dia.); creamy white candle wax; candlewick with metal tab; craft glue; and beaded, crocheted, or braided trim.

1. Using ivory paint, *Dry Brush* pot (page 181).

2. Follow manufacturer's instructions to melt wax. Dip wick tab in melted wax; place in pot, covering hole in bottom. Holding wick in place with a clothespin, fill pot with melted wax to ¹⁄₂" below rim; allow to set. Fill remainder of pot with melted wax to ¹⁄₄" below rim and allow to set. Trim wick.

3. Glue trim along outer rim of pot.

Tip

Add fragrance to your candles to "coordinate" with your beaded trims! If you are using green and red adornments for the holidays, try evergreen or cinnamon-spice. An animal print trim might go best with an earthy scent, while choosing a lush floral would compliment jewel-tone beads and golden trimmings.

FLOWERPOT FAVORS

(shown on page 82)

For each favor, you will need a small terra-cotta pot (ours measure approx. 3"h x 2 1/2" dia. and 3 1/2"h x 3" dia.), matte spray sealer, red and other assorted colors of acrylic paint, sponges, gold leaf kit, 1 1/2"w wired ribbon, small belt buckle or button (with large holes) larger than hole in bottom of pot, silk flower stem with leaves, hot glue gun, green floral tape, cellophane bag, wrapped candies, twist tie, liner paintbrush, 1 1/4" dia. key tag with split ring, 1" dia. circle paper punch, green card stock, and a black permanent fine-point marker.

Allow sealer and paint to dry after each application.

1. Cover pot completely with sealer.

2. *Sponge Paint* basecoat color onto outside and 1" inside top edge of pot (page 182).

3. Follow gold leaf kit manufacturer's instructions to apply adhesive size to pot (skipping some areas to allow base color to show through) and to complete gold leafing process.

4. Thread ribbon through belt buckle or button; place inside pot. Thread, then pull ribbon ends through hole in bottom of pot to the outside.

5. Cut flower stem to 9". Hot glue extra leaves below blossom, if needed; wrap stem with floral tape. Bend bottom 3/4" of stem at a right angle. Place stem inside cellophane bag, then place bag in pot. Fill bag with candy; gather bag around stem and close with twist tie.

6. Bring ribbon from bottom up around sides of pot; knot around bag at back, then tie into a bow at front.

7. For tag, paint a thin red circle along inside rim of key tag. Punch a circle from card stock; glue inside red circle. Use marker to write name on tag, then twist ring around stem of flower.

CUSTOM GIFT BAGS

(shown on page 83)

For each bag, you will need a white paper lunch bag, holiday-motif tissue paper, spray adhesive, decorative-edge craft scissors, gold and red permanent fine-point markers, gift to place in bag, hole punch, 18" length each of gold and red craft wire, white card stock, and assorted buttons.

1. Measure height of bag; subtract 2 1/2". Measure width of bag; subtract 1/2". Cut a piece of tissue the determined measurements.

2. Use spray adhesive to adhere tissue to front of bag. Trim top edges of bag with craft scissors.

3. Use gold marker to draw wavy lines around tissue on bag; use red marker to add dots along lines.

4. Place gift in bag, then fold top of bag down 1 3/4". Punch two holes, 1/4" apart, through folded section at center top of bag. Thread wire ends through holes from back to front; twist to secure.

5. For tag, cut a motif from tissue and adhere to card stock. Trim around motif 1/4" outside design. Use markers to embellish tag; punch a hole in top center of tag. Add tag and buttons to wires, then curl ends of wires to secure.

Tips

Any flower would look lovely in a pot gilded with gold leaf. Choose a basecoat paint color and ribbon that coordinates with your flower of choice to complete the project.

Other ideas to dress up plain paper bags for gift giving: holiday-motif wrapping paper, the top layer of a decorative napkin, or stickers. Select coordinating markers and craft wire to finish your presentations off in grand style!

GOURMET GIFTS FROM YOUR KITCHEN

DECORATED CANDY BOXES

(shown on pages 86 and 87)

For each box, you will need a white ready-to-assemble candy box, spray adhesive, holiday-motif tissue paper, ribbons, desired embellishments (we used a tinsel pom-pom and silk holly leaves) and purchased tags.

1. For paper-covered box, apply spray adhesive to right side of unfolded box. Smooth onto wrong side of tissue paper, then cut out along the edges and reassemble. Place wrapped gift in box and close box.

2. Embellish boxes as desired … wrap with ribbons, layered scrapbook paper strips, and ribbons, then add a tinsel pom-pom or silk leaves and a tag.

DECORATED CLAY POTS WITH TAGS

(shown on pages 88 and 89)

For each gift, you will need white spray primer, paintbrushes, small clay pot (ours measure 3"h x 4¼" dia.), clear cellophane bag to fit in pot, gift to place in bag, twist tie, and clear acrylic sealer.

Refer to Painting Techniques, page 180, before beginning project. Use hot glue for all gluing unless otherwise indicated. Allow primer, paint, and sealer to dry thoroughly after each application.

Hot Pepper Pot

You will need red, gold, silver, and green acrylic paint, ³⁄₈"w gold pleated ribbon, ³⁄₈"w silver wire-edged ribbon, tracing paper, cream card stock, and a hole punch.

1. Apply primer, then two coats of red paint to pot. Randomly *Dry Brush* gold and silver streaks on pot. Apply sealer to pot.

2. Place bag in pot, then gift in bag; seal bag with twist tie. Tie ribbons into a multi-loop bow around bag.

3. For tag, trace background and chile patterns, page 168, onto tracing paper; cut out. Use pattern to cut background from card stock. Draw around chile pattern onto center of background. Paint chile red and chile leaves and stem green; paint name on chile gold. *Dry Brush* gold and silver streaks across tag. Punch a hole at top of tag, then use a length of ribbon to attach tag to gift.

Beaded Pot

You will need gold acrylic paint, hot glue gun, beaded trim, green gimp trim, 2" x 3" piece of white card stock, hole punch, permanent marker, and 1½"w sheer wire-edged ribbon.

1. Apply primer, then two coats of gold paint to pot; apply sealer to pot.

2. Glue beaded trim around rim of pot, then glue gimp over beaded trim.

3. For tag, round corners on one end of card stock piece; punch a hole in tag. Glue beaded trim along bottom of tag, then glue gimp over beaded trim. Write name on tag; use tip of paintbrush handle to paint gold *Dots* on tag.

4. Place bag in pot, then gift in bag; seal bag with twist tie. Tie ribbon into a bow around bag; use a length of ribbon to attach tag to bag.

Silver Pot

You will need silver and pearl acrylic paint, ¹⁄₈"w silver wire-edged ribbon, hot glue gun, 2"w blue sheer ribbon, red and white card stock, decorative-edge craft scissors, craft glue stick, two teacup-shaped charms, and black and red permanent markers.

1. Apply primer, then two coats of silver paint to inside and outer rim of pot, then apply two coats of pearl paint to remainder of pot. Apply sealer to pot.

2. Wrap silver ribbon randomly around pot, spot gluing to secure.

3. Place bag in pot, then gift in bag; seal bag with twist tie. Knot blue ribbon around bag; cut ends into a V. Tie several lengths of silver ribbon into a multi-loop bow around bag.

4. For tag, cut a piece from red card stock; using craft scissors, cut a piece from white card stock and adhere to red piece using glue stick.

5. Hot glue charms to tag. Use black marker to draw steam above each charm and red marker to write message on tag.

Tip

Spruce up purchased tags with hand-drawn borders and holiday designs, then add a festive ribbon hanger.

TIN CONTAINERS AND TAGS

(shown on pages 88 and 89)

For each gift, you will need a tin container (ours measure 2³/₄"h x 3¹/₄"w at top), cellophane bag to fit in tin, gift to place in bag, and white card stock.

Fabric-Covered Container

You will need spray adhesive, fabric to cover tin, 12"w gold mesh ribbon, twist tie, 2¹/₂"w green sheer wire-edged ribbon, craft glue, narrow gold ribbon, metallic gold paint pen, two miniature gold ball ornaments, and gold cording.

Allow glue to dry after each application.

1. Using spray adhesive, cover entire tin with fabric.

2. Cut a length of mesh ribbon twice as long as cellophane bag. Place ribbon, then bag in tin; fill bag with gift and seal with twist tie. Gather mesh ribbon around bag, then knot a length of sheer ribbon around gathers.

3. For tag, cut two 1¹/₂" dia. circles from card stock, and one from fabric. Glue fabric circle to one card stock circle. For hanger, fold a short length of narrow ribbon in half and glue ends between card stock circles. Use paint pen to draw a border along edges and to write a message on back of tag.

4. Thread tag and ornaments onto a length of cording and tie to gift.

Paper-Covered Container

You will need spray adhesive, gift wrapping paper, hot glue gun, gold cording, fringed trim, stiff mesh fabric, twist tie, gold ribbon, craft glue stick, permanent marker, hole punch, and a metallic gold chenille stem.

1. Using spray adhesive, cover tin completely with wrapping paper.

2. Hot glue lengths of cording to paper on tin to accent designs. Hot glue fringe along rim on inside of tin.

3. Place a piece of fabric, then bag in tin. Fill bag with gift; seal with twist tie, then knot ribbon around bag.

4. For tag, cut a 1¹/₂" dia. circle from paper and card stock; matching wrong sides, use glue stick to glue pieces together, then write message on tag. Punch a hole in tag; use chenille stem to attach tag to gift.

Beaded Container

You will need thick craft glue, package of multi-color seed beads, blue handmade paper, twist tie, 1¹/₂"w red sheer ribbon, utility scissors, thin craft steel, permanent marker, and red cording.

1. Apply glue to one side of tin; sprinkle beads over glue and allow to dry. Repeat on all sides of tin.

2. Tear a piece of handmade paper large enough to fit in tin and cover cellophane bag. Place paper, then bag in tin. Place gift in bag, then seal bag with twist tie. Gather paper around bag, then knot ribbon around paper.

3. For tag, cut same-size spirals from steel and card stock and glue them together. Write message on card stock side of tag.

4. Apply glue to steel side of tag; sprinkle beads over glue and allow to dry. Use a length of cording to attach tag to gift.

MINI-LOAF BAG AND TAG

(shown on page 90)

You will need clear-backed red alphabet stickers, green card stock, decorative-edge craft scissors, double-stick tape, red paper gift bag, ¹/₂"w gold crinkled ribbon, gold corrugated kraft paper, wire cutters, green craft wire, assorted acrylic beads, paintbrush, ¹/₈" dia. hole punch, and a brass paper fastener.

1. Use stickers to spell out message on card stock. Cut out message, using craft scissors to cut bottom edge of paper. Tape message to bag.

2. Use tape to adhere two lengths of gold ribbon above and below message.

3. For tag, use stickers to spell out name on card stock. Cut out tag, trimming one end with craft scissors and cutting the opposite end to a point. Cut a star from kraft paper. Leaving a tail for attaching to bag, wrap a length of wire around star, adding beads and curling wire around a paintbrush handle to secure beads in place.

4. Place wrapped gift in bag; fold top of bag down 1¹/₂". Place pointed end of tag under fold; punch a hole through bag and tag. Insert fastener through hole and open prongs at back to secure. To attach star to bag, wrap tail of wire around fastener.

CHOOSE YOUR BAKING PAN

Standard Muffin Pan = ¹/₂ cup batter in each cup
Miniature Muffin Pan = 2 tablespoons batter in each cup
Jumbo Muffin Pan = slightly less than 1 cup batter in each cup
9 x 5-inch loafpan = 8 cups batter
8 x 4-inch loafpan = 4 cups batter
5 x 3-inch loafpan = 2 cups batter
9-inch square pan = 10 cups batter
8-inch square pan = 8 cups batter
13 x 9-inch rectangle pan = 12 to 15 cups batter
10-inch tube pan = 12 to 16 cups batter
Miniature tube pans = 1 cup batter in each mold

PAINTED CLAY PLATE AND TAG
(shown on page 90)

You will need a clay saucer (ours measures $1^1/8$"h x $6^1/2$" dia.), paintbrushes, red acrylic paint, gold paint pen, cellophane, wire-edged ribbon, craft glue stick, red gift wrapping paper, ivory card stock, decorative-edge craft scissors, gold corrugated kraft paper, wire cutters, gold craft wire, assorted beads, paintbrush, hot glue gun, and a $1/8$" dia. hole punch.

1. Paint saucer red; allow to dry. Use paint pen to paint designs along rim.

2. Place plastic-wrapped loaf on saucer, then place saucer on cellophane. Gather cellophane above saucer, then tie a length of ribbon around gathers; trim excess cellophane.

3. For tag, use glue stick to glue a piece of gift wrap to a piece of card stock. Use paint pen to outline edges of tag. Cut a star from kraft paper to fit on tag.

4. Wrap a length of wire randomly around star, adding beads and curling wire around a paintbrush handle to secure beads in place. Twist wire ends together at back to secure. Hot glue star to center of tag.

5. Punch a hole in corner of tag. Thread tag onto a length of wire and attach tag to gift.

MINI-MUFFIN BOX AND TAG
(shown on page 90)

You will need $1/4$" dia. brass nail heads, cardboard candy box with handle and cellophane window, gold corrugated kraft paper, wire cutters, gold craft wire, assorted glass beads, small paintbrush, hot glue gun, red gift wrapping paper, decorative-edge craft scissors, white vellum, large star rubber stamp, gold ink pad, and $1/4$" dia. red eyelets and an eyelet setter.

1. Punch evenly spaced nail heads into box around window on box.

2. Cut a star from kraft paper; wrap a length of wire randomly around star, adding beads and curling wire around a paintbrush handle to secure beads in place. Twist wire ends together at back to secure. Hot glue star to box.

3. For card, fold a $3^1/2$" x $6^1/4$" piece of gift wrap in half lengthwise. Cutting one long edge (top) straight and remaining edges with craft scissors, cut a 3" x $3^1/4$" piece from vellum; stamp star onto center of vellum piece. Matching top edges, center vellum on folded paper piece. Follow manufacturer's instructions to set eyelets 1" apart at top center of card. Thread a length of wire through eyelets from back, add beads and curl around paintbrush handle as desired; twist wire ends together to secure.

LOAF WRAPPER AND CARD
(shown on page 90)

You will need craft glue, 3"w red satin ribbon, $1/2$"w gold crinkled ribbon, wire cutters, gold wire, assorted beads, small paintbrush, red gift wrapping paper, seasonal rubber stamp, gold ink pad, and a gold paint pen.

1. Overlapping and gluing ends together at the bottom, wrap a length of red ribbon, then two lengths of gold ribbon around a plastic-wrapped loaf.

2. Cut a length of wire long enough to wrap around loaf twice. Wrapping wire around a paintbrush handle to hold beads in place as you go, add beads to wire. Stretching wire as necessary, wrap beaded wire around loaf, twisting ends together at top to secure.

3. For card, fold a 3" square of gift wrap in half. Stamp front of card, then use paint pen to write name.

LOAF BAGS AND GIFT TAGS
(shown on page 93)

Paper Bag

You will need four $1^3/8$" x $3^3/4$" manila tags, red thread, green and red handmade paper, four red miniature buttons, red-checked fabric, spray adhesive, $6^1/2$" x $13^1/2$" brown paper bag, two $1/4$" dia. red eyelets and an eyelet setter, and $1/8$"w green sheer ribbon.

1. Place three tags side-by-side; with one letter on each tag, use pencil to write "joy" across tags. Use sewing machine and red thread to sew over drawn letters.

2. (Note: For gift tag, sew leaves near hole in tag.) For each tag, tear three holly leaves from green paper. Arrange leaves on tags, then use red thread to sew a vein down center of each leaf. Sew a button at center of each set of leaves.

3. Cut a $5^1/4$" x $9^1/4$" piece of checked fabric and fringe ends. Tear a 6" x 10" piece of red paper. Center fabric piece on paper piece. Using a wide zigzag stitch, sew pieces together just inside fabric edges. Apply spray adhesive to wrong side of paper piece and adhere to center front of bag. Arrange and glue "joy" tags on top of fabric piece.

4. Place a plastic-wrapped loaf in bag, then fold top of bag 1" to back. Follow manufacturer's instructions to attach eyelets through all layers of fold. Lace ribbon through eyelets and tie ends into a bow.

5. Write a greeting on gift tag and attach to gift.

Fabric Bag

You will need a 13" x 16" piece of red-checked fabric, red embroidery floss, red miniature buttons, solid red fabric and muslin scraps, star rubber stamp, red ink pad, Design Master® glossy wood-tone spray, raffia, cream card stock, red handmade paper, and a craft glue stick.

Use a ½" seam allowance for all sewing. Use three threads of floss for all hand-sewing.

1. Matching right sides and long edges, fold checked fabric piece in half. Sew long edges together; press seam open. With seam at center back, sew one end closed.

2. Flatten bottom seam at each corner to form point. Sew across each corner 1" from point (Fig. 1). Turn bag right side out.

Fig. 1

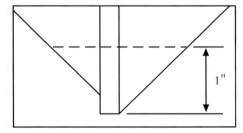

3. For cuff, fold top of bag 1½" to right side. Spacing evenly and sewing through both layers, sew buttons to cuff.

4. Cut a 3½" solid fabric square and a 3" muslin square; fray fabric edges. Stamp star design on muslin square; spray with wood-tone spray and allow to dry.

5. Use floss and buttons to attach layered squares to center front of bag.

6. Place plastic-wrapped loaf in bag; tie closed with raffia.

7. For tag, tear a 2" square each from card stock and handmade paper. Stamp star design on card stock; spray with wood-tone spray and allow to dry. Layer and glue squares together. Leaving floss long enough to attach tag to bag, sew a button to top corner of tag; tie tag to bag.

MUFFIN BAG AND TAG
(shown on page 93)

You will need red-checked fabric, brown lunch bag, green and red handmade paper, red floss, heart charm, four 6mm jingle bells, spray adhesive, seasonal rubber stamp, red ink pad, and a black permanent pen.

1. From fabric, tear a 3¼" x 3½" piece, and a 1"w strip to fit width of bag. Tear a 4½" x 6" piece from green paper, and a 2" x 2½" piece from red paper.

2. Use floss to tack charm and three bells to red paper piece. Glue red paper to fabric piece, then fabric to green paper piece; glue green paper piece to front of bag.

3. Place wrapped muffin in bag. Fold top of bag down 2¼", then glue fabric strip to flap.

4. For tag, tear a 1½" x 2¾" piece from green paper and a 2" x 3¼" piece from red paper; glue green piece to center of red piece. Stamp center of tag, then use pen to write name. Use floss to attach remaining bell to corner of tag; use floss to tie tag to gift.

PAINTED MUG WITH TAG
(shown on page 93)

You will need large and small star rubber stamps, red glass paint, liner paintbrush (if needed), packet of specialty coffee or several tea bags, clear cellophane, red raffia, red and brown handmade paper, craft glue stick, red ink pad, red floss, and two 6mm jingle bells.

1. Use star stamps and paint to decorate mug; randomly paint *Dots* on mug (page 181). Touch up designs with liner brush and paint if necessary. Follow glass paint manufacturer's instructions for curing paint.

2. Place coffee or tea, then a plastic-wrapped jumbo muffin in mug. Wrap entire gift in cellophane and tie closed with raffia.

3. For tag, glue a torn brown paper square to center of a torn red paper square; using ink pad, stamp a large star in center of tag. Using three strands of floss, sew bells to tag. Poke a hole in tag; use floss threaded through hole, to tie tag to gift.

PAINTED SNOWMAN PLATES
(shown on page 95)

For each plate, you will need tracing paper; 8" dia. clear plain glass dessert plate; removable tape; black, pink, orange, brown, red, and white glass paint; paintbrushes; matte clear acrylic spray sealer; and Design Master® Denim Home Décor Spray Stain.

Refer to Painting Techniques, page 180, before beginning project. Allow paint, sealer, and stain to dry after each application.

1. (*Note:* If needed, reduce or enlarge snowman pattern to fit plate). Trace pattern, page 167, onto tracing paper. Position pattern, right side down, on top of plate so that it shows through to bottom of plate (clip edges of pattern as necessary to ease onto plate); tape in place.

2. Paint black eyes, mouth, buttons, and stripes on hat; pink cheeks; orange nose; brown arms; red stripes, cuff, and pom-pom on hat, stripes on scarf, and words. Apply two to three coats of sealer to bottom of plate to prevent colors from bleeding.

3. Paint white snowman, scarf, stripes on hat, snowflakes, and *Dots*; remove pattern.

4. Follow manufacturer's instructions to spray bottom of plate with several coats of stain. Apply sealer to plate.

Patterns

Painted Snowman Plate
(page 166)

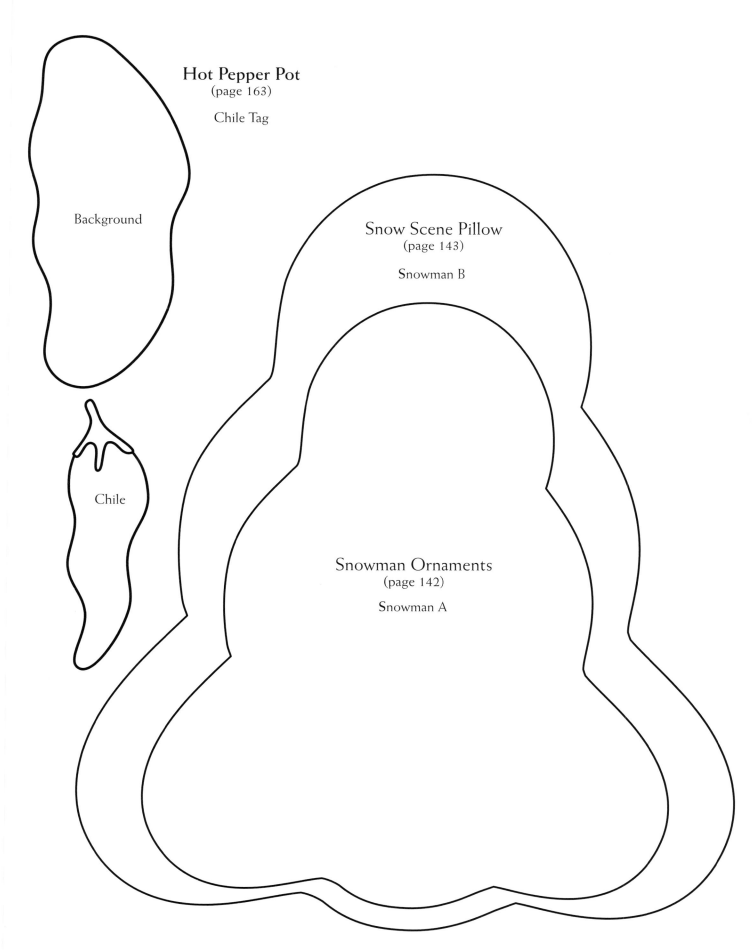

Hot Pepper Pot
(page 163)

Chile Tag

Background

Chile

Snow Scene Pillow
(page 143)

Snowman B

Snowman Ornaments
(page 142)

Snowman A

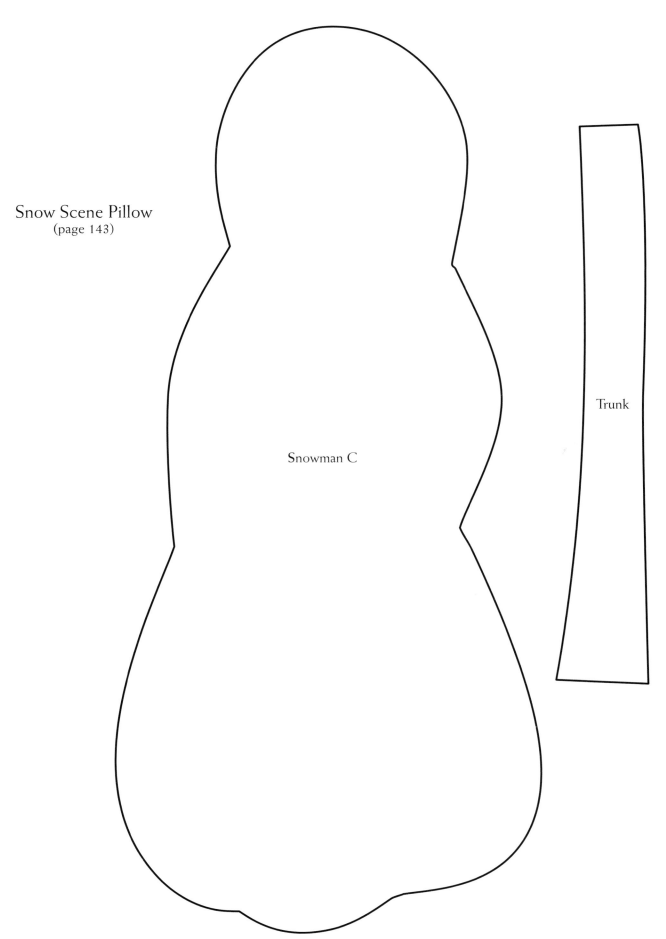

Snow Scene Pillow
(page 143)

Snowman C

Trunk

Felt Stars
(page 142)

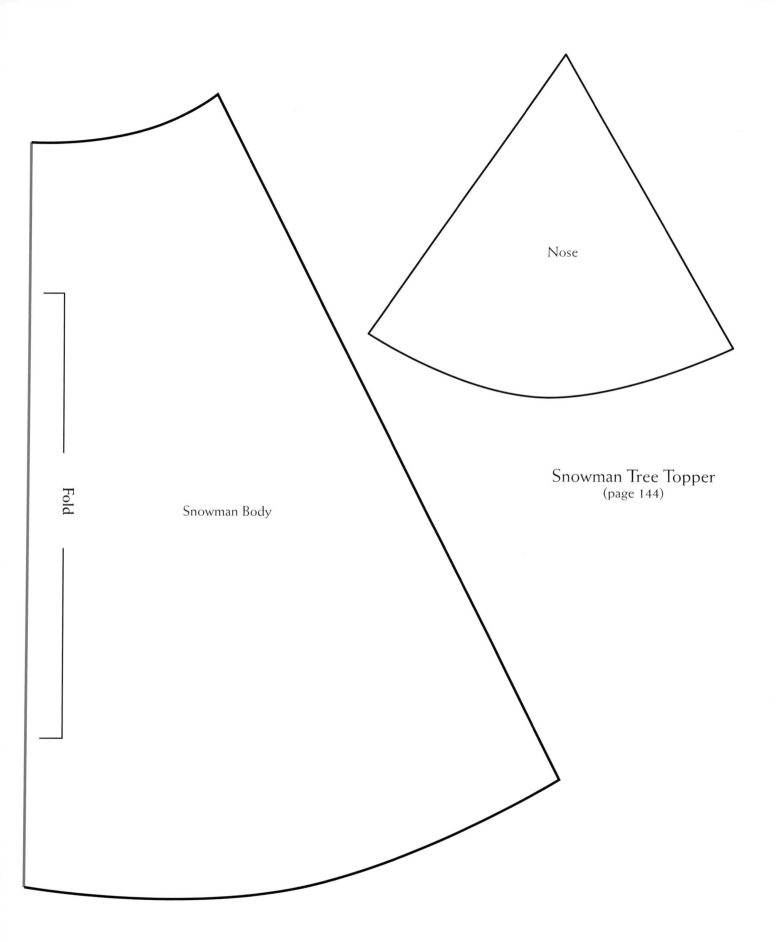

Nose

Snowman Tree Topper
(page 144)

Fold

Snowman Body

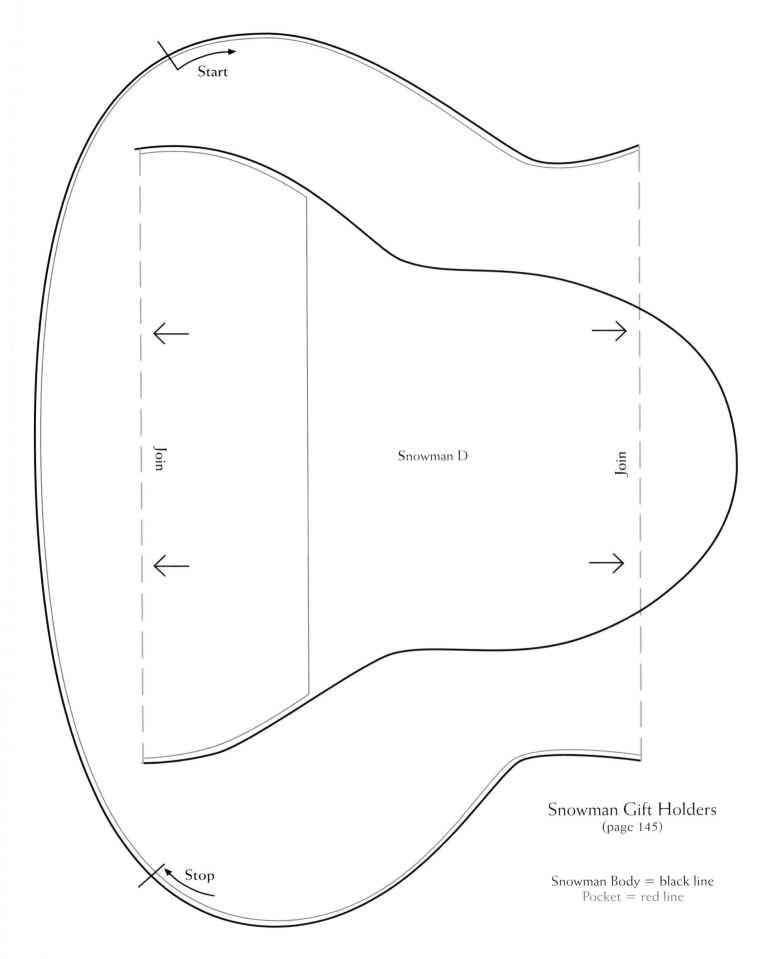

Start

Join

Join

Snowman D

Join

Join

Stop

Snowman Gift Holders
(page 145)

Snowman Body = black line
Pocket = red line

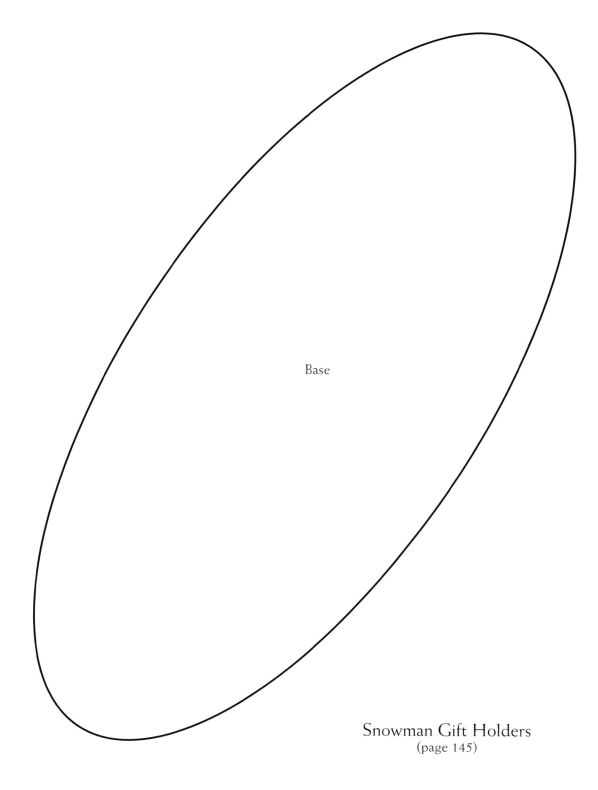

Base

Snowman Gift Holders
(page 145)

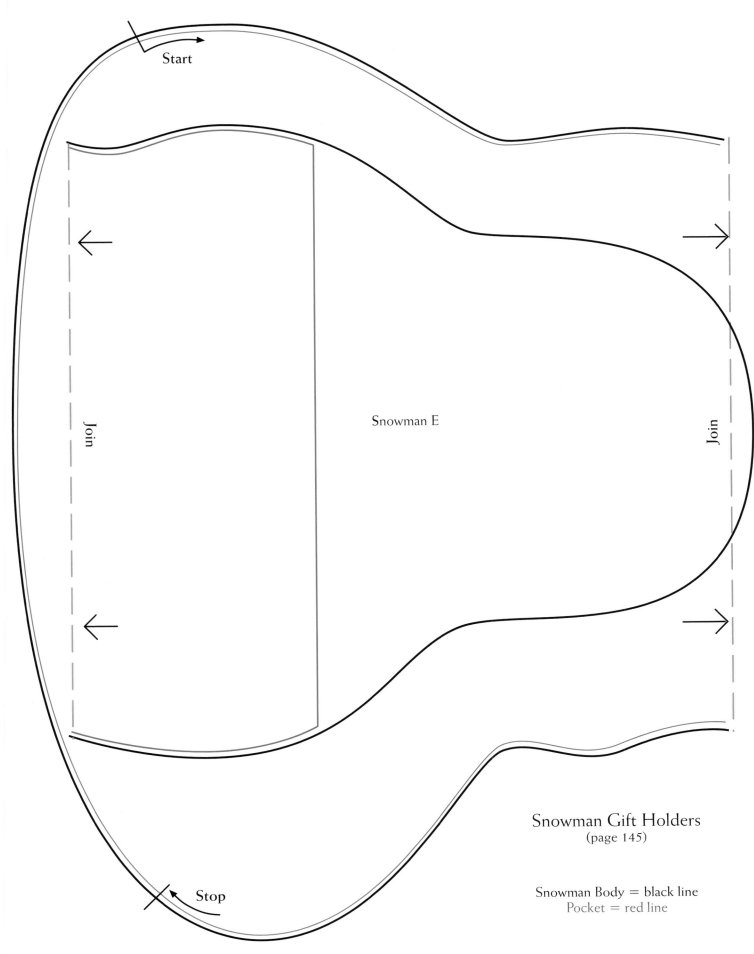

Start

Join

Join

Snowman E

Stop

Snowman Gift Holders
(page 145)

Snowman Body = black line
Pocket = red line

Leaves

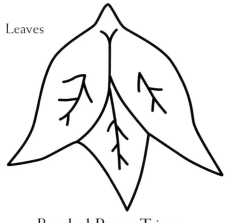

Beaded Paper Trims
(page 146)

Hat

Face

Mittens

Cookie Exchange Party

When:

Where:

Please RSVP with the name of the cookie you'll be bringing. Wrap some of your cookies... along with the recipe on one of the enclosed cards...for each guest. Bring extra cookies for snacking at the party.

Invitation

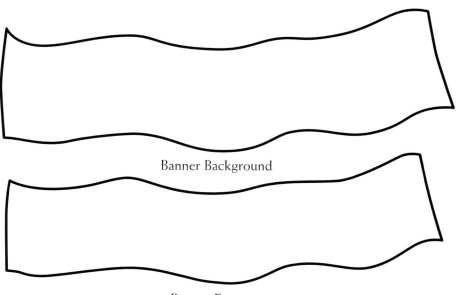

Banner Background

Banner Front

Invitation
(page 152)

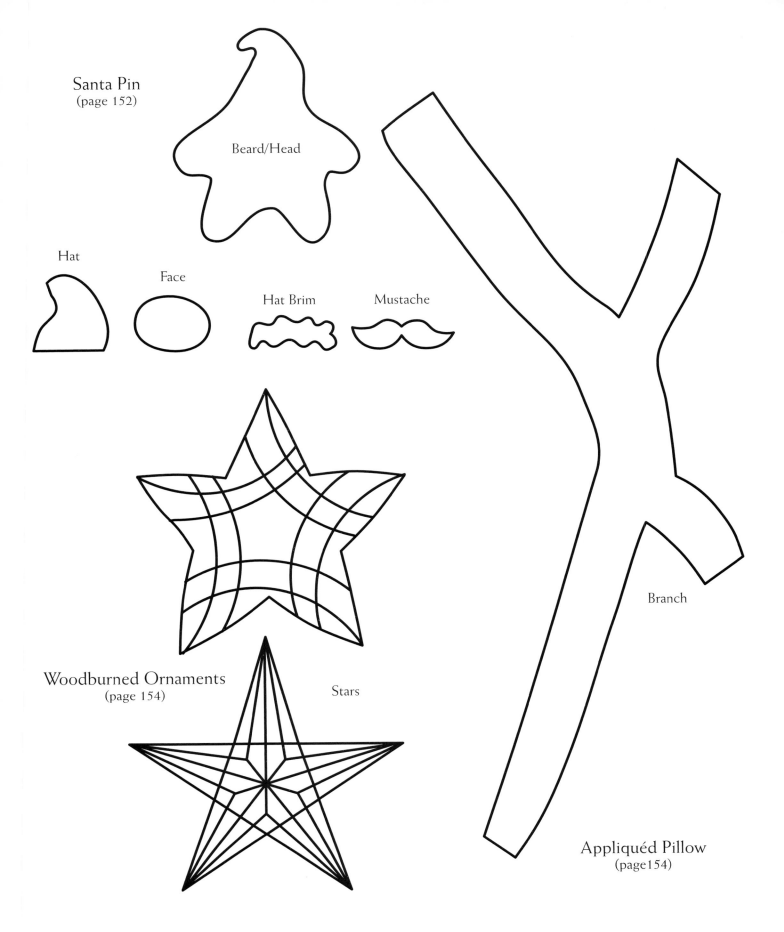

Santa Pin
(page 152)

Beard/Head

Hat

Face

Hat Brim

Mustache

Branch

Woodburned Ornaments
(page 154)

Stars

Appliquéd Pillow
(page 154)

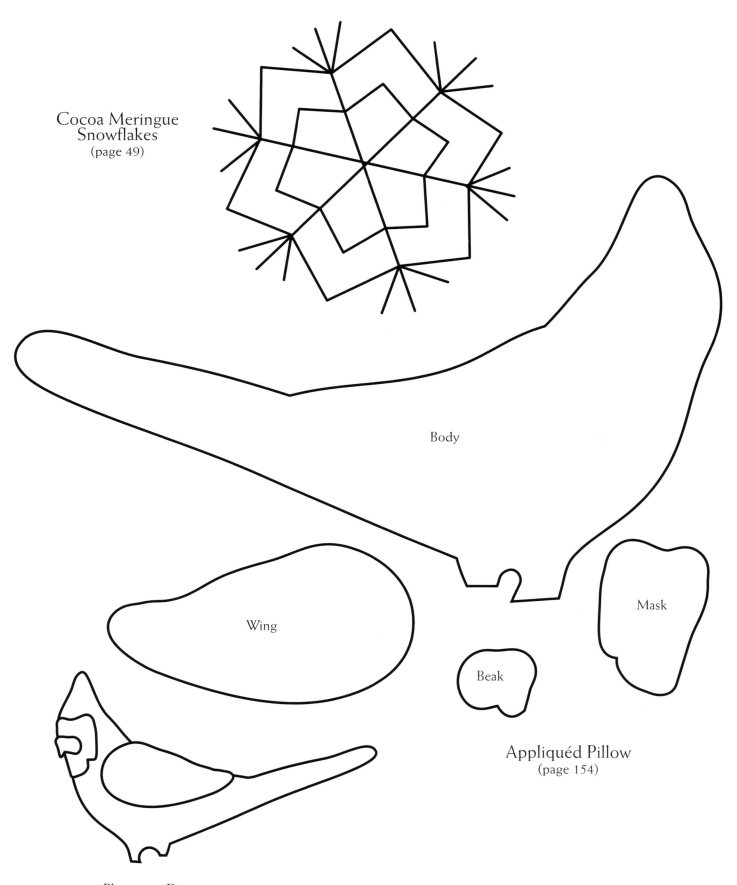

Cocoa Meringue
Snowflakes
(page 49)

Body

Wing

Mask

Beak

Appliquéd Pillow
(page 154)

Placement Diagram

Reindeer Placemats
(page 158)

Reindeer

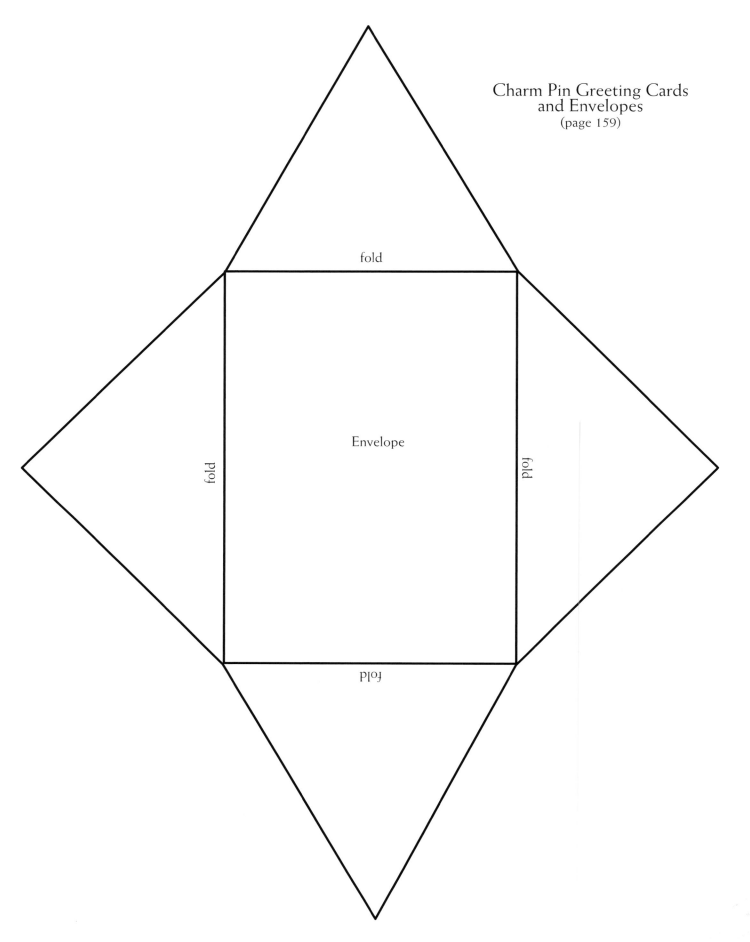

Charm Pin Greeting Cards
and Envelopes
(page 159)

fold

fold

Envelope

fold

fold

General Instructions

ADHESIVES

When using any adhesive, carefully follow the manufacturer's instructions.

White craft glue:
Recommended for paper. Dry flat.

Tacky craft glue:
Recommended for paper, fabric, florals, or wood. Dry flat or secure items with clothespins or straight pins until glue is dry.

Craft glue stick:
Recommended for paper or for gluing small, lightweight items to paper or other surfaces. Dry flat.

Fabric glue:
Recommended for fabric or paper. Dry flat or secure items with clothespins or straight pins until glue is dry.

Découpage glue:
Recommended for découpaging fabric or paper to a surface such as wood or glass. Use purchased découpage glue or mix one part craft glue with one part water.

Hot or low-temperature glue gun:
Recommended for paper, fabric, florals, or wood. Hold in place until set.

Jewelry or Gem glue:
Recommended for gluing jewelry and gems on fabric, plastic, wood, or florals. Dry flat or secure items in place until glue is dry.

Rubber cement:
Recommended for paper and cardboard. May discolor photos; may discolor paper with age. Dry flat (dries very quickly).

Spray adhesive:
Recommended for paper or fabric. Can be repositioned or permanent. Dry flat.

Household cement:
Recommended for ceramic or metal. Secure items with clothespins until glue is dry.

Wood glue:
Recommended for wood. Nail, screw, or clamp items together until glue is dry.

Silicone adhesive:
Recommended for ceramic, glass, leather, rubber, wood, and plastics. Forms a flexible and waterproof bond.

MAKING PATTERNS

WHOLE PATTERNS

When the whole pattern is shown, place tracing paper over pattern and trace pattern. For a more durable pattern, use a permanent marker to trace pattern onto stencil plastic.

TWO-PART PATTERNS

When tracing a two-part pattern, match the dashed lines and arrows to trace the patterns onto tracing paper, forming a whole pattern.

HALF PATTERNS

When only half of a pattern is shown (indicated by a solid blue line on the pattern), fold tracing paper in half. Place the fold along the blue line and trace pattern half; turn folded paper over and draw over traced lines on remaining side of paper to form a whole pattern.

Or, fold fabric in half. Trace pattern half onto tracing paper and cut out. Place "blue line" of pattern along fold in fabric and pin in place. Cutting through both layers, cut along black line(s) of pattern to cut out a whole pattern.

PAINTING TECHNIQUES

A disposable foam plate makes a good palette for holding a small amount of paint and mixing colors. It can easily be placed in a large resealable plastic bag to keep remaining paint wet while waiting for an area of applied paint to dry.

When waiting for a large area to dry before applying a second coat, wrap your paintbrushes in plastic wrap and place them in the refrigerator to keep the paint from drying on your brushes. Always clean brushes thoroughly after painting is complete, to keep them in good condition.

Following the manufacturer's instructions will produce the best results for any paint product. If you are unfamiliar with a specific painting technique, practice on a scrap of wood, cardboard, paper, or fabric before beginning project.

Work in a well-ventilated area and protect work surfaces with newspaper or a drop cloth.

TIPS FOR PAINTING ON FABRIC

If painting on fabric or a garment, wash, dry, and press item according to paint manufacturer's recommendations. To help stabilize fabric, insert a T-shirt form into a garment, pin fabric to a piece of foam core, or iron shiny side of freezer paper to wrong side of item under area to be painted. After painting, allow paint to dry before removing the stabilizing insert.

TRANSFERRING PATTERNS

Note: If transferring pattern onto a dark surface, use a light-colored transfer paper to transfer pattern.

Trace pattern onto tracing paper. Using removable tape, tape tracing paper pattern to project. Place transfer paper (or graphite paper), coated side down, between project and tracing paper. Use a stylus or pencil to lightly draw over pattern lines onto project.

TRANSFERRING DETAIL LINES

To transfer detail lines to project, using removable tape, tape tracing paper pattern to project. Place transfer paper (or graphite paper), coated side down, between project and tracing paper over painted basecoat and use a stylus or pencil to lightly draw over detail lines of pattern onto project.

ADDING DETAILS

Use a permanent marker or paint pen to draw over transferred detail lines or to create freehanded details on project.

PAINTING BASECOATS

A basecoat is a solid color of paint that covers the project's surface.

Use a medium to large paintbrush for large areas and a small brush for small areas. Do not overload brush. Allow paint to dry after each coat.

AGED OR DISTRESSED FINISH

This technique gives the project a faux-aged or distressed look.

Allowing to dry after each application, paint project the desired basecoat color. Randomly apply a thin layer of paste floor wax with a soft cloth or rub a candle over areas on project to be aged (such as the edges). Paint project the desired topcoat color and allow to dry. Lightly sand project to remove some of the paint, revealing the basecoat color in some areas. Wipe project with a tack cloth to remove dust, then seal with a clear acrylic sealer.

AGED METALLIC FINISH

This technique creates a faux-aged metallic finish on the project's surface.

Apply a rust-colored spray primer to the project and allow to dry. Next, *Sponge Paint, Method 2*, (page 182) an area of the project with orange, then brown paint; while paint is still wet, use a blow dryer to blow the paint across the surface as it dries. Repeat to cover the project as desired. Seal the surface with a clear matte sealer.

COLOR WASH

A color wash is a light coloration of a project's surface. It is similar to Dry Brush, yet creates a softer look that penetrates the surface.

To create a color wash, mix one part acrylic paint with two to three parts water. Dip paintbrush in color wash and brush across the area to receive the color. Decrease pressure on the brush as you move outward. Repeat as needed to create the desired effect.

CRACKLING

This technique creates a crazed effect on project surface, allowing the basecoat to show through the topcoat, which produces an aged effect.

Paint surface with desired basecoat color and allow to dry. Apply an even coat of crackle medium (the thicker the coat of crackle medium, the deeper the cracks). While paint is still tacky, but not dry, brush on one coat of a second paint color. Cracks will appear on the surface in the direction of the brush strokes.

There are a variety of crackle mediums available. One variety is applied over two layers of paint and another comes in colors and is applied over one layer of paint. Be sure to follow the manufacturer's instructions for the medium you choose.

DOTS

Dip a spouncer, dauber, round paintbrush, the handle end of a paintbrush, or one end of a toothpick in paint and touch to project. Dip item in paint each time for uniform dots.

DRY BRUSH

This technique creates a random topcoat coloration of a project's surface. It is similar to a Color Wash, yet creates an aged look that sits on top of the project's surface.

Do not dip brush in water. Dip a stipple brush or old paintbrush in paint; wipe most of the paint off onto a dry paper towel. Lightly stroke the brush across the area to receive color. Decrease pressure on the brush as you move outward. Repeat as needed to create the desired effect.

LINE WORK (permanent pen)

To prevent smudging lines or ruining your pen, let painted areas dry before beginning line work. Draw over detail lines with permanent pen.

LINE WORK (liner brush)

Mix paint with water to an ink-like consistency. Dip liner brush into thinned paint. Touch tip of brush to painting surface to outline details.

RUSTING

This technique gives the project's surface a faux-rusted finish.

1. Spray surface of project with a rusty-red color primer.

2. For paints, unevenly mix one part water to one part orange acrylic paint; unevenly mix one part water to one part dark orange acrylic paint.

3. (*Note*: To create a more natural rusted look, use a paper towel or a clean damp sponge piece to dab off paint in some areas after applying paint. Also, drip a few drops of water onto painted surface while paint is still wet, let them run, and then allow to dry.) Dip a dampened sponge into paint; blot on paper towel to remove excess paint. Allowing to dry after each coat, use a light stamping motion to paint project with orange, then dark orange paint mixtures. Apply sealer to project and allow to dry.

SPATTER PAINTING

This technique creates a speckled look on the project's surface.

Dip the bristle tips of a dry toothbrush into paint, blot on a paper towel to remove excess, then pull thumb across bristles to spatter paint on project. Repeat until desired effect is achieved.

SPONGE PAINTING

This technique creates a soft, mottled look on the project's surface.

Practice sponge-painting on scrap paper until desired look is achieved. Try using different sponge types, such as a natural sponge, a cosmetic sponge, and a household sponge, to create different appearances.

Method 1:

1. Dampen sponge with water; squeeze out excess.

2. Dip sponge into paint, then blot on a paper towel to remove excess paint.

3. Use a light stamping motion to paint project. Allow to dry.

4. If using more than one color of paint, repeat Steps 1 – 3, using a new sponge piece for each color.

5. If desired, repeat technique using one color again to soften edges or to lighten a heavy application of one or more paint colors.

Method 2:

Note: Using two (or more) colors of paint while the paints are still wet blends the colors together and creates a softer look. Clean sponges as needed to keep from creating a muddy look.

1. Dampen sponge with water; squeeze out excess.

2. Dip sponge into one color of paint, then blot on a paper towel to remove excess paint; repeat to add a second color to another part of the sponge.

3. Use a light stamping motion to paint project.

4. If using more than one color of paint, repeat Steps 1 – 3, using the same sponge or a new sponge piece for each additional color.

STENCILING

These instructions are written for multicolor stencils. For single-color stencils, make one stencil for the entire design.

1. For first stencil, cut a piece from stencil plastic 1" larger than entire pattern. Center plastic over pattern and use a permanent pen to trace outlines of all areas of first color in stencil cutting key. For placement guidelines, outline remaining colored area using dashed lines. Using a new piece of plastic for each additional color in stencil cutting key, repeat for remaining stencils.

2. Place each plastic piece on cutting mat and use a craft knife to cut out stencil along solid lines, making sure edges are smooth.

3. Hold or tape stencil in place. Using a clean, dry stencil brush or sponge piece, dip brush or sponge in paint. Remove excess paint on a paper towel. Brush or sponge should be almost dry to produce best results. Beginning at edge of cutout area, apply paint in a stamping motion over stencil. If desired, highlight or shade design by stamping a lighter or darker shade of paint in cutout area. Repeat until all areas of first stencil have been painted. Carefully remove stencil and allow paint to dry.

4. Using stencils in order indicated in color key and matching guidelines on stencils to previously stenciled area, repeat Step 3 for remaining stencils.

SEALING

If a project will be handled frequently or used outdoors, we recommend sealing the item with clear sealer. Sealers are available in spray or brush-on forms and in a variety of finishes. Follow the manufacturer's instructions to apply sealer.

Some projects will require two or more coats of sealer. Apply one coat of sealer and allow to dry. Lightly sand with fine-grit sandpaper, then wipe with a tack cloth before applying the next coat.

DÉCOUPAGE

1. Cut desired motifs from fabric or paper.

2. Apply découpage glue to wrong sides of motifs.

3. Overlapping as necessary, arrange motifs on project as desired. Smooth in place and allow to dry.

4. Allowing to dry after each application, apply two to three coats of sealer to project.

EMBROIDERY STITCHES

BACKSTITCH

Referring to Fig. 1, bring needle up at 1; go down at 2. Bring needle up at 3 and pull through. For next stitch, insert needle at 1; bring up at 4 and pull through. Continue working to make a continuous line of stitches.

Fig. 1

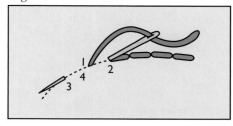

ADDING BEADS

Refer to project design and key for bead placement and sew bead in place using a fine needle that will pass through bead. Bring needle up at 1, run needle through bead and then down at 2. Secure thread on back or move to next bead as shown in Fig. 2.

Fig. 2

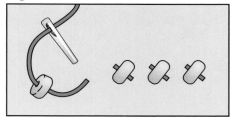

BLANKET STITCH

Bring needle up at 1. Keeping thread below point of needle, go down at 2 and up at 3 (Fig. 3). Continue working as shown in Fig. 4.

Fig. 3

Fig. 4

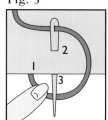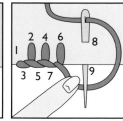

COUCHING

Lay thread to be couched on fabric. With second strand of thread, bring needle up at 1 and go down at 2. Continue making evenly spaced stitches along length of thread (Fig. 5).

Fig. 5

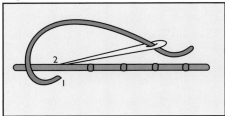

FRENCH KNOT

Bring needle up at 1. Wrap thread once around needle and insert needle at 2, holding thread with non-stitching fingers (Fig. 6). Tighten knot as close to fabric as possible while pulling needle back through fabric.

Fig. 6

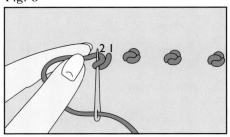

FEATHER STITCH

Bring needle up at 1; keeping thread below point of needle, go down at 2 and come up at 3 (Fig. 7). Go down at 4 and come up at 5 (Fig. 8). Continue working as shown in Fig. 9.

Fig. 7   Fig. 8

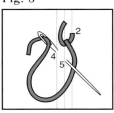

Fig. 9

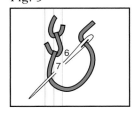

LAZY DAISY STITCH

Bring needle up at 1; take needle down again at 1 to form a loop and bring up at 2 (Fig. 10a). Keeping loop below point of needle (Fig. 10b), take needle down at 3 to anchor loop.

Fig. 10a   Fig. 10b

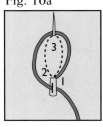 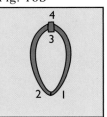

OVERCAST STITCH

Bring needle up at 1; take thread over edge of fabric and bring needle up at 2. Continue stitching along edge of fabric (Fig. 11).

Fig. 11

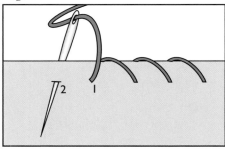

RUNNING STITCH

Referring to Fig. 12, make a series of straight stitches with stitch length equal to the space between stitches.

Fig. 12

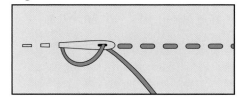

SATIN STITCH

Referring to Fig. 13, come up at odd numbers and go down at even numbers with the stitches touching but not overlapping.

Fig. 13

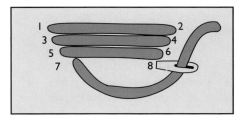

STEM STITCH

Referring to Fig. 14, come up at 1. Keeping thread below stitching line, go down at 2 and come up at 3. Go down at 4 and come up at 5.

Fig. 14

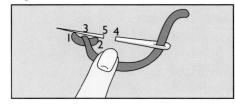

STRAIGHT STITCH

Bring needle up at 1 and take needle down at 2 (Fig. 15). Length of stitches may be varied as desired.

Fig. 15

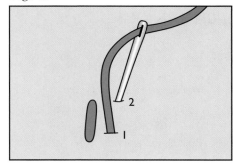

WHIPSTITCH

Bring needle up at 1 and take needle down at 2 (Fig. 16). Continue until opening is closed or trim is attached.

Fig. 16

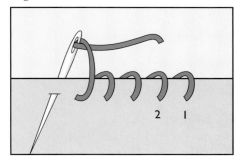

SEWING SHAPES

1. Center pattern on wrong side of one fabric piece and use fabric marking pen to draw around pattern. Do not cut out shape.

2. Place fabric pieces right sides together. Leaving an opening for turning, carefully sew pieces together directly on drawn line.

3. Leaving a 1/4" seam allowance, cut out shape. Clip seam allowance at curves and corners. Turn right side out and press. Sew opening closed.

CUTTING A FABRIC CIRCLE

1. Cut a square of fabric the size indicated in project instructions.

2. Matching right sides, fold fabric square in half from top to bottom and again from left to right.

3. Tie one end of string to a pencil or fabric marking pen. Measuring from pencil, insert a thumbtack through string at length indicated in project instructions. Insert thumbtack through folded corner of fabric. Holding tack in place and keeping string taut, mark cutting line (Fig. 1).

Fig. 1

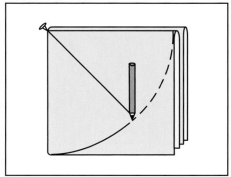

4. Cut along drawn line through all fabric layers.

FUSIBLE APPLIQUÉS

To prevent darker fabrics from showing through, white or light-colored appliqué fabrics may need to be lined with fusible interfacing before applying paper-backed fusible web.

To make reverse appliqué pieces, trace pattern onto tracing paper; turn traced pattern over and continue to follow all steps using the reversed pattern.

1. Use a pencil to trace pattern or draw around reversed pattern onto paper side of web as many times as indicated for a single fabric. Repeat for additional patterns and fabrics.

2. Follow manufacturer's instructions to fuse traced patterns to wrong side of fabrics. Do not remove paper backing.

3. Cut out appliqué pieces along traced lines. Remove paper backing.

4. Arrange appliqués, web side down, on project, overlapping as necessary. Appliqués can be temporarily held in place by touching appliqués with tip of iron. If appliqués are not in desired position, lift and reposition.

5. Fuse appliqués in place.

MACHINE APPLIQUÉ

1. Place paper or stabilizer on wrong side of background fabric under fused appliqué.

2. Beginning on a straight edge of the appliqué if possible, position project under presser foot so that most of stitching will be on appliqué. Take a stitch in fabric and bring bobbin thread to top. Hold both threads toward you and sew over them for several stitches to secure; clip threads. Using a medium-width zigzag stitch, stitch over all exposed raw edges of appliqué(s) and along detail lines as indicated in instructions.

3. When stitching is complete, remove stabilizer. Clip threads close to stitching.

BEADING BASICS

BEADING TIPS

Refer to the project supply list for each project to identify the types of beads and other supplies that we used.

We found that with some types of beads, such as "E" and seed beads, sizes may vary within a package, and the number of beads may need to be adjusted.

Place beads on a paper plate, bowl, or chamois cloth, or use the sticky side of several self-adhesive notes stuck together (to prevent them from curling). To keep from dropping beads, thread beads directly from the plate onto needle.

Pick up several beads on needle before moving them onto the thread. With practice, this is a real time-saver, too.

BEADING WITH THREAD

Choose from a variety of beading needles and threads to bead on fabric. We recommend that you work with beading thread, which is stronger than sewing thread. Be sure to use a size needle and thread that will pass through the smallest bead in your project without putting stress on the thread.

Threading Needle
Thread beading needle with one doubled strand of thread unless otherwise indicated in project instructions. It may be helpful to tape the tail to a table as you begin threading beads.

Locking Bead
A locking bead at the beginning of a strand keeps the beads from sliding off your thread. Leaving a 3" tail, string first bead on thread. Pass needle around and through bead again, to lock in place. Thread beads as indicated in project instructions. Locking beads are also used at the end of a thread or dangle.

Securing Thread Ends
To secure an ending thread, lock last bead in place and double back through last four beads; unthread needle, leaving a tail. Add new thread to continue strand (see *Adding Thread*, page 185), or trim tail and dot locking bead and thread end with liquid fray preventative; allow to dry.

To secure a beginning thread, rethread needle with beginning tail. Pass needle around locking bead and through next four beads. Trim tail and dot locking bead and thread end with liquid fray preventative; allow to dry.

Adding Thread

To add thread, pass newly threaded needle through the last three beads on the strand, leaving a 3" tail. Thread needle through last bead twice to lock in place and continue beading. Trim tails and dot locking bead and thread ends with liquid fray preventative; allow to dry.

BOWS

SIMPLE BOW

1. For the first streamer, measure and lightly mark 10" from one end of ribbon. For the first loop, begin at streamer mark; measure and lightly mark 8".

2. To form first loop, place first loop mark behind streamer mark; gather ribbon between thumb and forefinger (Fig. 1).

Fig. 1

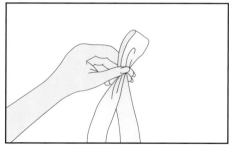

3. Loosely wrap remaining length of ribbon once around thumb (Fig. 2). To form second loop, fold remaining ribbon approximately 4" from end of wrapped area; slide folded end of ribbon through wrapped area.

Fig. 2

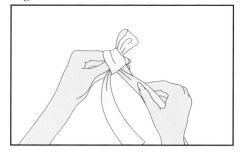

4. Place thumbs inside loops (Fig. 3). Pull the loops to tighten bow. Adjust size of loops by pulling on streamers. Trim streamers.

Fig. 3

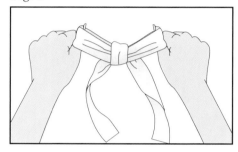

MULTI-LOOP BOW

Note: Loop sizes given in project instructions refer to the length of ribbon used to make one loop of bow. If no size is given, make loops desired size for project.

1. For first streamer, measure desired length of streamer from one end of ribbon; twist ribbon between fingers (Fig. 1).

Fig. 1

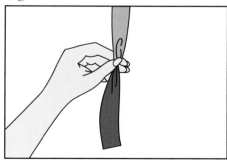

2. Keeping right side of ribbon facing out, fold ribbon to front to form desired-size loop; gather ribbon between fingers (Fig. 2). Fold ribbon to back to form another loop; gather ribbon between fingers (Fig. 3).

Fig. 2

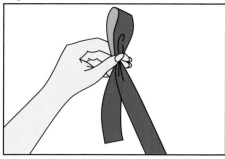

Fig. 3

3. (*Note*: If a center loop is desired, form half the desired number of loops, then loosely wrap ribbon around thumb and gather ribbon between fingers as shown in Fig. 4; form remaining loops.) Continue to form loops, varying size of loops as desired, until bow is desired size.

Fig. 4

4. For remaining streamer, trim ribbon to desired length.

5. To secure bow, hold gathered loops tightly. Fold a length of floral wire around gathers of loops. Hold wire ends behind bow, gathering all loops forward; twist bow to tighten wire. Arrange loops and trim ribbon ends as desired.

Kitchen Tips

MEASURING INGREDIENTS

Liquid measuring cups have a rim above the measuring line to keep liquid ingredients from spilling. Nested measuring cups are used to measure dry ingredients, butter, shortening, and peanut butter. Measuring spoons are used for measuring both dry and liquid ingredients.

To measure flour or granulated sugar: Spoon ingredient into nested measuring cup and level off with a knife. Do not pack down with spoon.

To measure powdered sugar: Lightly spoon sugar into nested measuring cup and level off with a knife.

To measure brown sugar: Pack sugar into nested measuring cup and level off with a knife. Sugar should hold its shape when removed from cup.

To measure dry ingredients equaling less than $1/4$ cup: Dip measuring spoon into ingredient and level off with a knife.

To measure butter, shortening, or peanut butter: Pack ingredient firmly into nested measuring cup and level off with a knife.

To measure liquids: Use a liquid measuring cup placed on a flat surface. Pour ingredient into cup and check measuring line at eye level.

To measure honey or syrup: For a more accurate measurement, lightly spray measuring cup or spoon with vegetable oil cooking spray before measuring so the liquid will release easily from cup or spoon.

SOFTENING BUTTER OR MARGARINE

To soften 1 stick of butter, remove wrapper and place butter on a microwave-safe plate. Microwave on medium-low power (30%) 20 to 30 seconds.

SUBSTITUTING HERBS

To substitute fresh herbs for dried, use 1 tablespoon fresh chopped herbs for 1 teaspoon dried herbs.

USING CHOCOLATE

Chocolate is best stored in a cool, dry place. Since it has a high cocoa butter content, chocolate may develop a grey film, or "bloom," when temperatures change. This grey film does not affect the taste.

When melting chocolate, a low temperature is important to prevent overheating and scorching that will affect flavor and texture. Use a dry spoon to stir chocolate while melting. When melted, remove from heat and use as desired. If necessary, chocolate may be returned to heat to remelt.

The following are methods for melting chocolate:

Chocolate can be melted in a heavy saucepan over low heat and stirred constantly until melted.

Melting chocolate in the top of a double boiler over hot, not simmering, water is a good method to prevent chocolate from overheating.

Using a microwave oven to melt chocolate is fast and convenient. Microwave chocolate in a microwave-safe container on medium-high power (80%) 1 minute; stir with a dry spoon. Continue to microwave as needed, stirring chocolate every 15 seconds until smooth. Frequent stirring is important, as the chocolate will appear not to be melting, but will be soft when stirred. A shiny appearance is another sign that chocolate is melting.

MELTING CANDY COATING

To melt candy coating, place in top of a double boiler over hot, not simmering, water or in a heavy saucepan over low heat. Stir occasionally with a dry spoon until coating melts. Remove from heat and use for dipping as desired. To flavor candy coating, add a small amount of flavored oil. To thin, add a small amount of vegetable oil, but no water. If necessary, coating may be returned to heat to remelt.

TOASTING NUTS

To toast nuts, spread nuts on an ungreased baking sheet. Stirring occasionally, bake in a 350° oven 5 to 8 minutes or until nuts are slightly darker in color.

PREPARING CITRUS FRUIT ZEST

To remove the zest (colored outer portion of peel) from citrus fruits, use a fine grater or citrus zester, being careful not to grate bitter white portion of peel.

WHIPPING CREAM

For greatest volume, chill a glass bowl and beaters before beating whipping cream. In warm weather, place chilled bowl over ice while beating whipping cream.

SOFTENING CREAM CHEESE

To soften cream cheese, remove wrapper and place cream cheese on a microwave-safe plate. Microwave on medium power (50%) 1 to $1^1/2$ minutes for an 8-ounce package or 30 to 45 seconds for a 3-ounce package.

SHREDDING CHEESE

To shred cheese easily, place wrapped cheese in freezer 10 to 20 minutes before shredding.

TESTS FOR CANDY MAKING

To determine the correct temperature of cooked candy, use a candy thermometer and the cold water test. Before each use, check the accuracy of your candy thermometer by attaching it to the side of a small saucepan of water, making sure thermometer does not touch bottom of pan. Bring water to a boil. Place thermometer in water for 10 minutes. Thermometer should register 212°. If it does not, adjust the temperature range for each candy consistency accordingly.

When using a candy thermometer, insert thermometer into candy mixture, making sure thermometer does not touch bottom of pan. Read temperature at eye level. Cook candy to desired temperature range. Working quickly, drop about 1/2 teaspoon of candy mixture into a cup of ice water. Use a fresh cup of water for each test. Use the following descriptions to determine if candy has reached the correct stage:

Soft-Ball Stage (234 to 240°): Candy can be rolled into a soft ball in ice water but will flatten when removed from water.

Firm-Ball Stage (242 to 248°): Candy can be rolled into a firm ball in ice water but will flatten if pressed when removed from water.

Hard-Ball Stage (250 to 268°): Candy can be rolled into a hard ball in ice water and will remain hard when removed from water.

Soft-Crack Stage (270 to 290°): Candy will form hard threads in ice water but will soften when removed from water.

Hard-Crack Stage (300 to 310°): Candy will form brittle threads in ice water and will remain brittle when removed from water.

EQUIVALENT MEASUREMENTS

1	tablespoon	=	3	teaspoons
1/8	cup (1 fluid ounce)	=	2	tablespoons
1/4	cup (2 fluid ounces)	=	4	tablespoons
1/3	cup	=	5 1/3	tablespoons
1/2	cup (4 fluid ounces)	=	8	tablespoons
3/4	cup (6 fluid ounces)	=	12	tablespoons
1	cup (8 fluid ounces)	=	16	tablespoons or 1/2 pint
2	cups (16 fluid ounces)	=	1	pint
1	quart (32 fluid ounces)	=	2	pints
1/2	gallon (64 fluid ounces)	=	2	quarts
1	gallon (128 fluid ounces)	=	4	quarts

HELPFUL FOOD EQUIVALENTS

1/2	cup butter	=	1	stick butter
1	square baking chocolate	=	1	ounce chocolate
1	cup chocolate chips	=	6	ounces chocolate chips
2 1/4	cups packed brown sugar	=	1	pound brown sugar
3 1/2	cups unsifted powdered sugar	=	1	pound powdered sugar
2	cups granulated sugar	=	1	pound granulated sugar
4	cups sifted all-purpose flour	=	1	pound all-purpose flour
1	cup shredded cheese	=	4	ounces cheese
3	cups sliced carrots	=	1	pound carrots
1/2	cup chopped celery	=	1	rib celery
1/2	cup chopped onion	=	1	medium onion
1	cup chopped green pepper	=	1	large green pepper

Recipe Index

Recipe Index continued on page 190.

Project Index